AEROFILMS GUIDE

The Leeds–Liverpool Canal

Colin Speakman

IAN ALLAN
Publishing

THE LEEDS-LIVERPOOL CANAL

Based on an original idea by
Richard Cox of Aerofilms

Designers Michael D. Stride and
Robert G. Wilcockson
Series Editor Rebecca King

Published by Ian Allan Ltd, Shepperton, Surrey;
and printed at their works at Coomblands in
Runnymede, England

Text © Ian Allan Ltd 1993
Photographs © Aerofilms 1993

First published 1993

ISBN 0 7110 2135 X

Contents

Inset: Kildwick
Main picture: Wheelton
Title page: Bank Newton

Other titles in this series:

The South Downs Way

The South Devon Coast Path

The Cotswold Way

The Thames Path

Offa's Dyke (South) and the River Wye Valley

SECTIONS OF THE PATH

The route from Liverpool to Leeds has been divided into sections that can be tackled in a day (see Some practical points, page 6). Each of these sections opens with an introduction and the distance involved is given.

GENERAL TEXT

Places to visit, points of interest and information relevant to that particular stretch of the canal accompanies every photo-map. Always check details of opening times in advance of a visit. Generally, opening times are limited between October and Easter.

DIRECTION

In general, the right-hand edge of the photo-map joins the left-hand edge of the map on the next spread. However, to make the direction of the route absolutely clear where it twists and turns, arrows indicate how the maps link together.

SYMBOLS

The following symbols appear on the photo-maps for information and to help the walker get his bearings.

Railway station
Place of interest
Pub or hotel
P Car park
Church
The route

Following

Following the Leeds-Liverpool Canal is easy as long-distance walks go and thanks to the British Waterways

Steeton & Silsden to Shipley
11 miles (17.5km)

Breakpoint: Bingley

This day's walk goes through Airedale, through what might be described as classic West Riding country – mills, moors, stone walls and green valley – which even though blighted by modern industry and a high-speed road which is to all intent and purpose a motorway, has the craggy heights of open moors above to give a sense of space and grandeur. A number of massive glacial moraines not only give the valley floor a surprisingly undulating character, but cause the river to serpentine between low hillocks – unlike the canal which takes a more direct, elevated route, contouring along the edge of the hillside.

Getting to Steeton & Silsden
Frequent MetroTrain services (Airedale Line) from Leeds, Bradford Forster Square, Keighley and Skipton serve Silsden Station – Sundays included. Motorists should park at Steeton & Silsden Station (large free car park) and return by train.

SILSDEN, ALTHOUGH much expanded in recent years as modern commuter estates have spread along the hillsides, is still a typical stone-built Pennine town at heart. A stream

with an accompanying chorus of ducks runs alongside the winding main street, and there are some attractive 18th- and 19th-century cottages and shops, an early 18th-century church and Victorian chapel, a meeting room and cottages, as well as mill buildings alongside the canal. A choice of cafés and pubs offer refreshment.

116

The vertical photography used in the photo-maps is taken from an average height above sea level. This means that the scale of the photography will alter slightly as the contours of the ground vary. The photo-maps are constructed by piecing together a series of photographs to make each page. They are intended to give a

the Route

and various local authorities the towpath is generally well maintained.

Warehouses alongside the canal at Silsden indicate the town's industrial past

THE ROUTE

The canal curves past farms and swing bridges towards Silsden, its modern housing developments covering the hillside before the older part of the town, with its wharfs and marina, is reached. Keep ahead to the bridge carrying the A6034 where steps lead up to the village centre to the left.

It's about ¾ mile to Steeton & Silsden Station, though an alternative is to catch a bus (services 712, 762 or 765) from near the canal bridge which will stop on the overpass above Steeton Station or allow you to carry on into Keighley. There are frequent trains (Sundays included) to Keighley, Leeds and Bradford, and back to Skipton or Gargrave.

OBLIQUE PHOTOGRAPHS
These photographs bring a new perspective to the landscape and its buildings. All the subjects chosen can be seen from, lie on, or are within easy reach of the towpath.

THE ROUTE
In general, the route follows the canal towpath and is very straightforward. Now and again, numbers and letters are inserted into the text which correspond to the numbers and letters in yellow on the photo-maps.

VERTICAL PHOTO-MAPS
Every step of the route is plotted on vertical photographs using a scale of 1:10,000 (0.6 miles:3.9ins, 1km:10cm).

COMPASS POINT
Every photo-map is accompanied by a compass point for ease of orientation.

SCALE FOR PHOTO-MAPS
The scale-bar represents a distance of 0.310 miles (0.5km).

pictorial representation of the ground and strict accuracy of scale throughout cannot be guaranteed. There may also be a mismatch in areas of extreme relief – ie where the land is steepest. These problems have been kept to a minimum, in particular close to the main route of the walk.

INTRODUCTION

The 127-mile (203km) long Leeds-Liverpool canal which crosses from the centre of Liverpool across the high Pennines to the centre of Leeds is both a national monument and a working waterway of immense and continuing social and economic value to the communities it serves.

The towpath is a superb long-distance footpath, as this book demonstrates, easy to follow and easy to enjoy. Above all it is accessible, on foot, by bike, by car and in most areas along the corridor by extremely good public transport.

It is interesting to note that apart from a few small sections, the towpath of the Leeds-Liverpool Canal is not a public right of way but is technically a permissive route, that is the public are invited to use it at the Board's discretion.

In real terms this means that it is open, but the BWB ask that walkers take care not to interfere with any canalside equipment or do anything that will spoil the pleasure of other users of the canal, including anglers.

Cycling is permitted along the canal with a BWB permit priced £3 and available from BWB offices.

Some practical points
It seemed to us that most people would want to walk the route not as backpackers, but in day stages, leaving home each day and walking another section before returning to a home base in the evening. The Leeds-Liverpool is almost perfect for this, served as it is by the rail network throughout its entire length. In many cases – in Merseyside, along the Douglas and Calder Valleys in Lancashire and thorough Airedale in North and West Yorkshire – the canal actually goes parallel to a railway line. These lines are not only open but carry busy commuter traffic from strategically position local stations, many of them extremely close to the canal. It therefore made sense to plan this book around the rail network. Eleven day stages have been devised, varying in length form 10

Left: Liverpool's Liver Building, near the start of the walk

Above: Wheelton Locks. The engineering feats of the canal builders are one of the attractions of a walk along the towpath.

to 15½ miles (16-25km), all linked to and from specific railway stations. This means that there is transport in the morning and back at the end of the afternoon without worrying about being picked up or needing two cars and two drivers. Details of each day's transport links, are given. Instructions are given for motorists as well as for public transport users. For each day stage, a suggested parking point is made from where motorists can either catch a train or bus back to their car, or perhaps take the train at the start of the day to walk back to their vehicle, the latter saving the need to consult timetables or wait about at the end of a walk.

Whilst even 15 miles (24km) of fairly level towpath is easily within the capabilities of most fit adults, we felt it necessary to give users the opportunity to have a useful 'breakpoint' about half-way along the route each day, say between 5 or 8 miles, (8 or 13km) so that a longer stage could be divided into two shorter days, again with a convenient train or bus available at the half-way point.

Backpackers will have little trouble finding accommodation outside the main city centres, which tend to only have larger hotels offering business standard (and business priced) accommodation. The answer might be to

choose places such as Ormskirk or Burscough on the Lancashire side or Skipton or Gargrave on the Yorkshire side to return to base each evening. It may also make sense for people wanting to do the whole walk to stay overnight in the areas furthest from home to save time and rail fares – or petrol.

No special equipment is need to walk a canal towpath. Old clothes and stout shoes are perfectly adequate, but most people will want their usual rambling gear, and given the climate on both sides of the Pennines this will include some warm clothing and waterproofs – and perhaps even a folding umbrella which can be surprisingly efficient in even the heaviest rain. Footwear is important as a continuous walk along any towpath, especially the sections where it is hard-surfaced, can be punishing on the feet. Lightweight boots or thick-soled trainers are adequate in drier weather. However, during or after wet weather, muddy stretches of the towpath (and there are several of those) can result in wet feet which usually means sore feet over any distance. Always carry spare food and drink with you although the canal has more than an average share of excellent canalside inns (a real temptation for the walker) and there is usually a pub by a railway station. Canalside marinas usually have shops and sometimes a café which walkers can use.

A rucksack is by far the best way to carry food and rainwear, and between October and March a torch is a good idea in case of delay at the end of an afternoon.

Stanley
Dock

③

A5036

②

Moorfields

James Street

①

River Mersey

Maritime
Museum

Albert
Dock

Liverpool (James Street Station) to Old Roan

10 miles (16km)

Breakpoint: Seaforth & Litherland

The first 2 miles (3.2km) of the walk, before you join the accessible section of the canal towpath, penetrates the centre of a great city still dominated by vast merchant shipping offices and warehouses. Once on the towpath to Bootle, the route goes through a typical urban landscape with a mixture of older, decaying industries and small-scale manufacturing and service enterprises.

Getting to James Street Station

If you are arriving in Liverpool by Inter-City or Regional Railways train services, take the MerseyRail Underground from Lime Street Station two stops to James Street. Motorists should park at Old Roan or at any station on the Ormskirk line and travel in by train rather than parking in central Liverpool.

THE ROUTE

From James Street (1), take the exit signed Water Street, leaving by the long, gradually ascending tunnel. On reaching Water Street the famous waterfront buildings, including the Liver and Cunard Buildings, and terminus of the Mersey Ferries, can be seen to the left. (To enjoy the waterfront and the views across the Mersey to Birkenhead, turn left and cross the road either by the overbridge or the traffic lights, keeping straight ahead for Pierhead and the Mersey Ferries. To the left is Albert Dock and the Maritime Museum.)

Turn right along Water Street past the India Buildings and the town hall as the street becomes Dale Street. On the left are the Rigby Buildings, dating from 1726, and on the right the terracotta and brick of the Prudential Assurance buildings of 1866. Turn left here towards Moorfields Station.

At the end of this street is the site of the old Exchange station, with the Lion Tavern on the street corner. Turn right, but take the street immediately next left, Pall Mall, marked by the Bradford Hotel on the corner.

Along Pall Mall (2), there are large brick Victorian warehouses, some of which have been carefully restored. Cross Leeds Street (the name recalling the canal it once served) at the traffic lights to continue up Pall Mall. On the right is a large warehouse serving several major national breweries. Some of these buildings were originally owned by the Leeds-Liverpool Canal company, and provided trans-shipment facilities before goods and raw materials were sent across the Atlantic or inland along the canal system. The factories on the right produce sacking for packaging and office furniture. To the right, at the next crossroads (Chisenhall Street), is the original bridge at the end of the Liverpool basin on the Leeds-Liverpool the canal; now the basin has been filled in the and the land occupied by new houses. On the left vacant land is being reclaimed by the Merseyside Development Corporation.

Continue over the next crossroads, passing small repair workshops dealing with a variety of items ranging from cookers to cars under the old railway arches. Go straight across the next junction, marked by a sub-station.

The road narrows as it follows the railway arches to gates. Take the last road left under the arch to join the A565, Great Howard Street (3). Turn right, passing in front of the massive tobacco warehouse and grain silo. Look for the plaque on the wall opposite which tells you you are standing on the bridge over Stanley Dock.

Take the next turning right, along Lightbody Street. Pass under the railway again and continue up to the canal bridge.

THE ROUTE

Descend steps to the canal towpath (1) where the start of the canal is marked by a milepost stating Leeds is 127 miles (203km) away. Boats can actually travel as far as Burlington Street a few hundred yards to the right, which now forms the canal's western terminal basin.

Also on your right, but reached by turning right again around the corner, are the Liverpool Locks which descend into Stanley Docks and down to the Mersey, although the towpath is blocked by the road. However, Birkenhead and the Mersey can still be seen from the top of the locks.

Retrace your steps back to the milepost to begin your walk along the canal. The Merseyside Watersports Centre is passed on Athol Street on the left. The area to the right is largely residential, with flats and modern low-rise housing forming part of the southern outskirts of Bootle.

After a short distance, the canal passes under Sandhills Lane (2), with Sandhills MerseyRail station near by – frequent services operate from here back to central Liverpool.

Rows of Victorian terraced houses now appear on the right, the railway crossing the canal at Kirkdale as the canal passes a muddle of old warehouses, haulage firms and second-hand car yards. In the middle distance can be seen Liverpool's extensive docks and, across the river, the docks and cranes of Birkenhead.

Part of Liverpool's famous 7-mile long waterfront on the River Mersey that is occupied by a network of dock complexes - many of which are now redundant

Bank Hall

Sandhills

②

①

Where the canal passes under a railway (1), a glance over the brick retaining wall will, in clear weather, give a fine long-distance view across the Mersey to the end of the Wirral peninsula.

The canal now runs through Bootle with more modern housing appearing and with the huge Girobank tower block dominating the skyline. In the town centre many of the canal approaches have been carefully renovated and landscaped. More modern houses give way to the Williams toffee factory, announced by its chimney, and the Sefton Council Highway Maintenance Depot. On the left, at Linacre, is a huge gas works complex.

BOOTLE, AN IMPORTANT port and manufacturing centre, was always independent from Liverpool and now forms part of the Borough of Sefton which extends along the Merseyside coast as far as Southport. Like Liverpool, it enjoyed dramatic growth from the early years of last century when a village of less than 1,000 people expanded to 78,000 by the middle years of the present century through a combination of ship-building, docks, warehousing and heavy industry. The large gas works at Linacre originally provided coal gas from vast quantities of coal bought by canal from the Lancashire coal fields. The canal and its towpath, close to the town's main shopping centre, now form an attractive central green corridor and heritage feature in Bootle.

The football stadium with Stanley Park beyond

Seaforth &
Litherland

A5660

Linacre

A5098

Bootle
New Strand

Toffee
Factory

BOOTLE

①

A5057

Bootle
Oriel Road

WHERE THE A5036 crosses the canal by a high-level bridge at Litherland there used to be a unique, electrically operated lift bridge. Built in 1922 to replace an earlier, inadequate wooden bridge, the bridge used complex machinery to raise the road deck out of the way to allow the passage of boats. As traffic increased on the main road during the 1960s and 1970s it became a notorious place for traffic jams, leading to its replacement by the present road bridge in 1975.

THE ROUTE

The canal enters an area dominated by factories, tower blocks and lines of terraces. It passes two schools and soon runs past a strongly smelling tar distillery (1) and goes under the A5036 (Church Road). An exit at this point leads to Seaforth &

Litherland Station on the Southport MerseyRail line – 6 miles (9.6km). Now the residential landscape becomes completely postwar, and the density of housing lessens with semi-detached housing and gardens dominating the landscape.

By Sefton Tannery, at Litherland, the canal crosses into the Rimrose valley with pleasant open fields and recreational grounds to the left, and a glance back gives views, on a clear day, across to the distant Clwydian Hills in Wales.

Liverpool's futuristic concrete and glass Roman Catholic cathedral, designed by Sir Frederick Gibberd, at one end of Hope Street

As the canal crosses under the B5422, Gubsey Lane (1), it makes its first real attempt at taking an easterly direction. The housing changes to medium rise blocks and three-storey flats as you approach Netherton. There are picnic benches and a small picnic area at Fleetwood Lane bridge. More modern semi-detached housing estates are reached at Netherton, as the density of housing decreases further, and the landscape opens up a little again with views to the north as the canal swings round Liverpool's urban fringe.

THE RIMROSE VALLEY is the first real open countryside reached on the journey from Liverpool. It takes its name from the little Rimrose Brook which flows southwards towards the Mersey. This is an area noted for its garden allotments – at one time there were 32 acres (13ha) of allotments as well as 37 acres (15ha) of local-authority-owned recreation land which provided a badly needed lung for heavily populated north Merseyside.

The city's Anglican cathedral - the largest in the world - stands at the other end of Hope Street. It is built of pink sandstone

A milepost (1) states you are now 8 miles (12.8km) from the start at Liverpool Locks (119 miles/190km to Leeds) before passing under the busy A5036. (The next bridge is the railway; take the next exit after this, on to the A59 (A), to get to Old Roan and the MerseyRail station. MerseyRail Northern line trains provide a frequent services from Old Roan back to central Liverpool.) Continue under the A59 bridge and along the towpath, with the old village of Aintree, now a busy suburb, to the left. The canal soon passes the northern tip of Aintree Racecourse on the right (now fenced in).

Aintree Racecourse

Old Roan to New Lane

15½ miles (25km)

Breakpoints: Maghull, Downholland Cross, Scarisbrick Bridge, Pinfold

The route between Old Roan and New Lane is the longest suggested day stage along the Leeds-Liverpool Canal and where, after the densely populated central and suburban areas of Liverpool and Bootle, the walker finds himself in remote and relatively unpopulated countryside, passing through that extensive area of rich, low-lying farmland that forms the West Lancashire Plain. It is during this stage, too, that the first good views of the now not-so-distant Pennines can be had.

Getting to Old Roan
Take the frequent MerseyRail Northern Ormskirk branch from Liverpool Central or Moorfields Station (Underground) to Old Roan Station.

Motorists should either park at Old Roan or, to take advantage of easier parking at Burscough Junction, travel to Old Roan by MerseyRail via Ormskirk.

Aintree Racecourse, home of the Grand National - the great steeplechase race that causes emotions among racing enthusiasts to run high because of the enormous fences

HOME OF THE Grand National, one of the world's most famous (and most notorious) steeplechase races, Aintree Racecourse lies alongside the Leeds-Liverpool Canal.

The canal has actually played a colourful part in the history of the Grand National. One of the bends on the difficult and demanding course is known as Canal Turn and until 1951, when the course was fenced to reduce trespass and damage, it was possible to watch the race from a barge on the canal, and a well-positioned barge was considered to be an excellent vantage point.

Horses even occasionally ran off the course and fell into the canal. There are tales of how, in years gone by, bookmakers who refused to pay out their dues were seized by their angry and disgruntled punters and ducked into the conveniently situated canal. During the inter-war years, when filming rights of the race were jealously protected, there is an account of an unsuccessful film company stealing a march on its rivals by illicitly filming the race from a slowly moving canal barge loaded with bundles of hay, the cameraman concealed inside the hay.

THE ROUTE

Continuing along the towpath by the edge of Aintree Racecourse (1), the canal now swings northwards around the edge of Aintree and crosses over the little River Alt before going under the M57. The railway to the right is the main Liverpool-Wigan line, whilst the large conurbation to the right forms part of Kirby, a large Merseyside suburb and Liverpool overspill area. Beyond the motorway (2) more open countryside appears as the canal curves back westwards towards Maghull.

WADDICAR

M57

River
Alt

① ②

②

STRADDLING THE CANAL, Maghull is an old town which, although gradually developed into a Merseyside commuter area, has kept something of its old flavour. The church was built in the 19th century, and the far older Chapel of St Andrew, going back seven centuries, stands near by. In the parish records there is an interesting entry relating to the canal: '1827: Packet fare from Maghull to Wigan of a sick woman 1s 10d (9p)'.

The little village of Sefton, which has given its name to the modern Metropolitan District, lies about 2 miles (3.2km) to the south-west of Maghull.

The canal winds its way through Maghull, an old town that has become swamped with new development

THE ROUTE

Keep ahead under the pylons, passing under Ledsom's Bridge (1), and with the little village of Melling with its 15th-century church on a slight rise to the right. Continue under a bridge, the concrete arches of the M58, and the railway bridge carrying the MerseyRail Northern line to Maghull and Ormskirk.

The canal now goes through the centre of Maghull, a town which straddles the canal. (To leave to return by train, take the next exit on the left (A), for Maghull town centre and the MerseyRail station.)

Continue along the towpath, once again going under the A59 trunk road (2) and heading northwards towards Lydiate.

St Catherine's Chapel ruins

① A567

LYDIATE IS ANOTHER village along the canal which has grown considerably in recent years as a dormitory area, the canal now defining its eastern boundary. About ½ mile north of the town are the ruins of the 15th-century Chapel of St Catherine, built for the Ireland family of Lydiate Hall. When the chapel fell into ruin, the pulpits and several carvings were removed to the nearby Catholic church.

The Scotch Pipers Inn near Lollies Bridge (no 17A) over the canal dates from the 14th century and is reputedly the oldest in Lancashire.

The 500-year-old ruins of St Catherine's Chapel, north of Lydiate

THE ROUTE

Gradually canal and towpath leave the outskirts of Maghull, skirting the edge of Lydiate and entering the West Lancashire Plain. The waterway now curves eastwards under the main A567 Southport road north of Lydiate (1), entering rich, almost flat countryside of scattered farms and prosperous market gardens that thrive on the dark peaty soils and mild West Lancashire climate protected from harsh easterly and northerly winds by the Pennines.

ORMSKIRK HAS BEEN a market town for some 700 years. Its church of St Peter and St Paul has a tower and a separate spire and it is thought likely that the tower was added to house bells brought from Burscough Priory after the Dissolution.

THE ROUTE

Canal and towpath curve round once again to make their way north-westwards past more scattered farmsteads and market gardens with their large, open fields. This is a landscape of far horizons and long views. Just beyond the second road bridge (1) the canal crosses the county boundary from Merseyside into Lancashire, entering the West Lancashire District. The low hills to the east are Clieves Hills, a notable viewpoint, and further east still lies the old town of Ormskirk.

At Downholland Cross there is a busy crossroads with a popular pub by the bridge, the Scarisbrick Arms. Bus services from here operate to both Maghull and Southport for MerseyRail connections.

Downholland Cross. The Scarisbrick Arms is the red-brick building on the left-hand side of the road

The canal goes through the edge of the attractive village of Haskayne before heading north-eastwards. Canal and towpath cross pleasant, open countryside. It is mainly arable farmland, but during the summer and early autumn a variety of vegetables such as cabbages, sprouts and leeks are grown. The canal keeps parallel with the A567 under a series of arched bridges carrying minor roads and farm tracks towards outlying farms and smallholdings.

ORIGINALLY A NORSE settlement, the small West Lancashire community of Haskayne retains much of its rural character, including the Ship Inn, a typical canalside tavern. About ½ mile west of Haskayne and accessible from the lane to Barton (A) is a linear nature trail. It follows a 1½-mile (2.4km) long cutting along a former branch railway from Southport to Saltcar and Hillhouses which closed in 1952. Managed by Lancashire Trust for Nature Conservation, the reserve is noted for its variety of wild plants, including marsh orchids and several species more usually associated with the coast or uplands. More than 60 species of orchids have been noted here. There is a waymarked trail through the reserve.

Haskayne lies to the left of the canal as it continues across flat arable land

Halsall
Cutting

(A)

A567

HASKAYNE

A567

HALSALL

A

①

HALSALL'S VILLAGE CHURCH, dedicated to St Cuthbert, is reputed to be the oldest church in Lancashire with parts of its structure perhaps dating back to 1290, and though extensively rebuilt, it retains much of its character. The village grammar school dates from 1593 and was endowed by Edward Halsall, a wealthy local landowner. Tombs of several of the Halsalls are still to be seen in the church.

THE ROUTE

The canal goes a short distance to the east of Halsall, with the Sacaracen's Head pub close by the village church. Lanes from Halsall (A) lead directly to Ormskirk about 3 miles (4.8km) due east, another possible place to terminate this stage of the walk.

Halsall, with St Cuthbert's Church on the right. At one time the 16th-century choir vestry was a grammar school

Victorian Scarisbrick Hall is now a private school

B5242

HEATON'S
BRIDGE

campsite

THE ROUTE

The canal now bears sharply eastwards under Scarisbrick
Bridge (1) on the A570 by Pinfold. If you've had enough by this
point, there are frequent buses from here to Southport and
Ormskirk. At Scarisbrick (2) (views of the Hall), the route
passes by woods and campsites before going under Heaton's
Bridge on the B5242 where there is an inn of the same name.

N

PINFOLD OWES ITS NAME to the time
when cattle-stealing was rife between
local landed gentry; a pinfold was a
small enclosure where lost or stolen
cattle could be reclaimed. The village
was also a popular refreshment halt on
the Liverpool-Southport route during
stage-coaching days. Scarisbrick Bridge
at Pinfold was a popular day excursion
destination in pre-railway days when
trippers came out by packet boat from
Manchester and Liverpool, with a shuttle
service of horse-drawn carriages taking
people on to Southport. This service only
ceased in the 1840s, when the railway
was opened through to Southport.

Reference to Scarisbrick Hall goes
back as far as 1328 when the Scarisbrick
family were already occupying a hall on
the same site where they remained until

1948. Sir Henry Scarisbrick was one of
Henry V's soldiers knighted at
Agincourt. His descendant, Charles
Scarisbrick, who died in 1860, was
reputed to be the richest commoner in
the whole of England.

Scarisbrick Hall, in its splendid estate,
visible from the canal, is a masterpiece of
Victorian architechture – neo-Gothic at
its most flamboyant. It was designed by
two of the most eminent architects of the
day, Augustus Welby Pugin (of Houses
of Parliament fame) and his son Edward.
Scarisbrick Hall is now a private school,
but is open to the public on one day each
year – look out for local announcements.

The half-timbered Hurleston Hall near
Hurleston Green to the south is
Elizabethan and is reputed to have both
a ghost and a priests' escape tunnel.

Martin Mere Wildfowl and Wetlands Centre, at Tarlscough

New Lane

Martin Hall

MARTIN MERE WILDFOWL and Wetlands Centre lies half an hour's walk from New Lane Station. This lakeland and marshland area was once far more extensive than at present. It was largely drained and transformed into agricultural land by Thomas Eccleston of Scarisbrick with the help of canal engineer John Gilbert in 1787. In order to fertilise the newly drained marshes, vast quantities of night soil – sewage – were brought from Liverpool and other towns in Lancashire along the canal. Small wharves are still visible by bridges along the canal where the night soil was loaded on to carts for scattering on the land.

The surviving 350 acres (141ha) of marshland and lake are now part of a strictly protected nature reserve, and form one of Britain's finest wildfowl centres. Among birds to be seen are flamingoes, many varieties of geese, Berwick swans, ducks, plovers and waders of all kinds. There are watching hides from which to observe birds as well as acres of gardens, nature trails, picnic areas and a play area for children. A fine Scandinavian- style visitor centre with a unique turfed roof has a lecture theatre and coffee shop. Exhibition areas provide a welcome to the centre and encourage the appreciation of birds and wildfowl. There are also excellent educational facilities for children and school groups. The centre is open most days of the year, but for obvious reasons dogs are not admitted.

THE ROUTE

From the bridge carrying New Lane over the canal (1) (where there is another pub), it is just ¼ mile to the left to the level-crossing to New Lane railway station. However, do check your train times in advance, as services calling at this station are infrequent, and it may be better to walk the extra 1½ miles (2.4km) to Burscough Bridge for more frequent trains on the Southport-Wigan-Manchester line or to Burscough Junction on the line to Ormskirk.

New Lane to Wigan Pier

13 miles (21km)

Breakpoints: Parbold, Appley Bridge

This day's walk starts from the West Lancashire Plain and heads into the first of the Pennine foothills, taking advantage of the valley of a little Lancashire river which itself played no small part in the early history of the canal, the River Douglas. River, canal and railway share this narrow valley before passing under the M6 into the outskirts of Wigan, a town like many others on the foothills of both sides of the Pennines. Here the coal measures lie relatively close to the surface, allowing fortunes to be made out of coal and coal-mining and providing a source of cheap energy. Though the coal mines have now closed and other industries such as engineering and textiles have diminished in importance, Wigan now enjoys an unexpected new lease of life as one of the North's most popular tourist centres.

Getting to New Lane
New Lane Station lies on the Manchester-Wigan-Southport line. If no suitable train is operating (there is no Sunday service) alight at Burscough Bridge, 1½miles to the west. Burscough Junction Station on the Ormskirk-Preston line (connections to and from Liverpool Central) is only slightly further away.

Burscough is well known to the boating fraternity as a good place to replenish supplies

BURSCOUGH WAS FOR many years something of an inland port, home to many working boatmen whose cottages, with stables for canal horses, are still evident. The Admiral Lord Nelson pub on the main bridge by the canal was the original 'Packet House' and was the staging post for regular passenger boat services between Liverpool and Wigan.

It is now an important centre for leisure boating with many busy moorings and facilities, including overnight accommodation, with a range of colourful converted barges and leisure cruisers usually to be seen.

THE ROUTE

Continue along the towpath into Burscough with its complex of wharves, moorings, warehouses, boat chandlers, canalside cottages and gardens, as well as another popular inn, the Farmers' Arms. Note the impressive mill on the right. Keep ahead under the railway bridge (1) carrying the Ormskirk-Preston railway. After less than ½ mile, meet the Rufford branch of the canal (2) and swing bridge past the Top Locks, the first of a series of seven handsome locks which take the canal down to Rufford and on to Tarleton towards the Ribble estuary.

Sewage Works

Canalside inns like the Ring o' Bells at Hoscar are popular with walkers, boatmen and tourists alike

THE RUFFORD BRANCH of the canal, completed in 1781, feeds into the tidal sections of the River Douglas at Tarleton. It was built to replace the lower reaches of the Douglas Navigation. Until 1800 access into the Douglas was at a lock at Sollom, but the canal was extended using the old river bed. This section is only accessible by boat, even the towpath having disappeared.

Rufford Old Hall, about 4 miles (6.4km) along the Rufford Branch (accessible by train from Burscough Junction), is a magnificent 15th-century half-timbered country house. Now owned and managed by the National Trust, it is a rare example of a house built around a medieval timber-framed hall. Furnished in ways which reflect its period, there are displays of armour and weapons, and of the life of a domestic servant as well as gardens and a café.

THE ROUTE

Keep ahead along a pleasant, well-maintained section of towpath to and beyond the Ring o' Bells pub at Hoscar (1) (bridge 24), before curving gradually northwards under more bridges towards the main Manchester-Southport railway line.

N

NEWBURGH, ONE OF several conservation areas in West Lancashire, has a large and particularly attractive green with a cross, a 17th-century coaching house and a village inn – the Red Lion.

Parbold was a small farming village for many centuries until the coming of the Douglas Navigation and the canal. Its water-powered flour mill on the Douglas was replaced by the windmill still standing today, which in turn was replaced by a steam-powered mill in the mid-19th century. Several attractive cottages survive in the village, as do handsome villas built for prosperous Lancashire merchants and manufacturers who, from the 1850s onwards, could commute to Parbold from as far as Manchester by fast stream train.

THE ROUTE

The canal now enters the beautiful Douglas valley (1). The village of Newburgh lies along the opposite bank from the towpath, accessible by lane and tunnel. Cross the viaduct which carries the canal over the River Douglas at Parbold. From this point onwards the canal and its towpath follow the river into Wigan. Keep ahead underneath the overbridge. Parbold Station is a mere hundred yards to the left of the bridge, as is the village centre. Note the old windmill tower to the right, and an old grain mill on the left. There is an impressive view of Parbold Hill ahead.

At the main bridge carrying the A5209 over the canal at Parbold (2), the towpath crosses to the right-hand bank of the canal for the first time since leaving Liverpool. Continue along to the edge of Parbold Hill.

The prettiest part of Parbold lies near the canal bridge; elsewhere is swamped with new building

A5209

Prior's Wood Hall

Appley Locks

PARBOLD LIES ON the edge of the South Lancashire coal field and coal of a poorer quality than that found on the rich upper coal measures in the Wigan area was mined from the lower coal measures which come close to the surface in this area. Gillibrand Colliery on the banks of the canal has long since vanished, but in the late 18th century a number of deep shafts were sunk, the workings extending underneath the canal. Water seeping into the workings was pumped out by steam engine, the coal being loaded directly on to barges on the canal.

Away to the right as you look across from the canal is a squat tower on the hilltop. This is Ashurst Beacon, erected on the site of a medieval beacon by Lord Skelmersdale in 1798 when a French invasion of Britain led by Napoleon seemed a distinct possibility.

Just before Appley Bridge you reach the first set of locks on the main canal since Liverpool, the end of a 27-mile (43km) open pound. There are a curious twin set of locks here. The first 12ft-lock is the original one, but two shallower locks were built in later years to reduce the amount of water consumed and to speed up traffic.

THE ROUTE

Canal, River Douglas and railway now share a narrow section of valley below Parbold Hill, the towpath running along an attractive stretch between river and canal, a fascinating juxtaposition of canal and railway tunnels and cuttings. Continue past Appley Locks and on to Appley Bridge which also has a pub and a railway station. Beyond Appley the canal enters Greater Manchester – the Wigan Metropolitan Borough.

Appley Locks. A second pair was built some time after the original, to speed up traffic

APPLEY BRIDGE HAS three adjacent bridges
over river, canal and railway. As you approach
on the towpath, there is a pub, the Navigation,
on the right, and the railway station on the left.
Both Appley and Shevington Vale are areas
where considerable housing development has
occurred in recent years. Large amounts of coal
were brought in former times from the local
pits by rail wagons around Shevington to be
carried onward by barge to Liverpool for
domestic consumption. Dean Locks at Gathurst
are another place where coal was loaded on the
canal, this time by tramway from Orrell mines
where Lancashire's first steam locomotives
were in use as early as 1813. Roburite Explosive
Works on the other side of the Gathurst M6
viaduct manufactured safe explosives for use in
coal mines.

The M6 crosses the canal just past Dean Locks outside Gathurst

THE ROUTE

Canal, river and railway now swing southwards towards Wigan, the towpath still between canal and river, with attractive areas of woodland across the valley, rich in wildlife. The M6 now dominates the skyline, and one's eardrums.

Just beyond Dean Locks (1), with its delightful lock-keeper's cottage, is the huge, level Gathurst Viaduct carrying the Anglo-Scottish motorway northwards and forming the highest complex of motorway, railway and canal bridges crossing the Douglas valley. Sadly, with the motorway so close, the intrusive noise of heavy traffic is continually present.

At Gathurst itself, almost immediately east of the viaduct, is another railway station on the Wigan line, only a short distance from the canal. Canal and river now bear away to the north of the railway and follow a slightly meandering line past an old explosive works. Go under the old works branch line towards Crooke.

CROOKE, A FORMER colliery village with traditional miners' cottages, has been carefully restored and the Crooke Hall inn by the canalside makes a pleasant place of refreshment.

Coal from nearby John Pit was loaded here and carried by barge to Liverpool's main gasworks to be used in the manufacture of town gas. Coal was the only source of gas until the coming of natural gas from the North Sea in the 1960s. This traffic continued until 1964, being the last regular freight traffic along the main line of the Leeds-Liverpool Canal. The stub of a former branch of the canal into the mine has recently been partly reopened to provide new moorings.

Just beyond Eli Meadow Lock (1) is the site of the former Pagefield Iron Works where for many years steam locomotives, colliery winding engines and similar heavy machinery related to the mining industry were built.

THE ROUTE

Continue past another small area of attractive woodland before reaching the village of Crooke. The canal now goes through semi-open countryside, the industrialised outskirts of Wigan becoming more dominant. Once under the railway bridge carrying the Southport line, the landscape becomes very much more urban in character. Keep directly ahead towards the centre of Wigan.

Wigan Pier was originally a small staithe at the centre of the town where barges were loaded with coal from a local pit

Wigan Wallgate

Wigan North Western

Leeds Liverpool West Office

Wigan Pier

Wigan to Chorley
13½ miles (22km)

Breakpoint: Adlington

This section of the canal has a quite different feel to the initial sections within Merseyside and West Lancashire, with steep hillsides and vast moorland summits now defining the horizon to the east as the high West Pennine moors are circumnavigated by the canal.

Beyond Wigan the first serious ascent into the Pennines has to be tackled, with an extended series of no less than 23 locks lifting the canal 200ft over less than 2 miles (3.2km) from Wigan canal basin.

From the summit of the Wigan flight of locks the canal turns northwards towards Adlington and Chorley, curving around the edge of Wigan and rejoining the Douglas valley, past Haigh Park.

Getting to Wigan

There are frequent train services from Wigan Wallgate Station to Southport and Manchester, whilst services from Wigan Northwestern link Liverpool with Wigan, Chorley, Preston and the West Coast main line. Motorists should park at Preston or at Bolton and take a train to Wigan, returning by frequent train from Chorley after completing the day's walk. As there are no direct trains from Chorley to Wigan this will save time and waiting for connections at the end of the day.

WIGAN HAS A long history, strategically situated as it was along the important highway between London and Scotland and becoming, along with Preston, Lancaster and Liverpool, a borough as long ago as 1246 when King Henry III granted each of the towns a charter. But it was coal, iron-making and textiles during the Industrial Revolution that developed the busy town we see today, supported by such trades as the manufacture of pottery, brass and pewter. From the late 18th century onwards, when both canal and railways linked the town directly with Liverpool, the town prospered. The canal enabled bales of American cotton to be brought direct off the trans-Atlantic ships to the new coal-powered mills and finished goods to be sent out to the expanding Empire. Much of the present attractive town centre with its pedestrianised areas and fine public buildings and shops dates from from Wigan's greatest period of prosperity in the middle and later years of last century when there were no less than 63 collieries at work, as well as countless cotton mills and iron works and steel-making plants.

Wigan Pier is the centre-piece of a group of old warehouses and mill buildings which have been carefully restored and transformed into a major Heritage Centre. A waterbus links attractions on the canal, and there are canal and nature trails to follow, plus gardens to visit.

THE ROUTE

A mixture of swampy, reedy ground and industry now dominate the route into the centre of Wigan. Keep directly ahead under a complex of railway and road bridges to Wigan Pier itself.

It is only a short walk along the main road, Wallgate, up the hill into town from Wigan Pier to either of Wigan's two stations – Wigan North Western which has direct services to Liverpool and Preston as well as Inter-City services, and Wigan Wallgate with local trains back to New Lane, Burscough or onwards to Bolton and Manchester.

B5238

Wigan Locks

A577

The long flight of Wigan Locks. Each lock is only 62ft long which means the longer, traditional narrowboats from the Midlands cannot use the canal west of Wigan

THE LEIGH BRANCH (7 miles / 11km long) was opened in 1820 to provide a link from the Leeds-Liverpool Canal to Manchester via the Bridgewater Canal which also had a branch. The branch linked Leigh with Wigan and Liverpool but also served the surrounding area, which was rich in coalfields. The branch carried the last regular commercial traffic along the canal, the transport of coal between Bickershaw Colliery and Wigan Power Station, which only ceased in 1972. Extensive mining in this area also resulted in serious earth movement and subsidence which in turn caused flooding and the creation of typical 'flashes' or small lakes. Several of these are to be seen adjacent to the Leigh branch. One of these, Pennington Flash, near Leigh, is now an important nature reserve, nationally known for its bird life, as well as being a country park.

Wigan Locks were built to connect the Leeds-Liverpool Canal's Wigan basin with the existing southern portion of the Lancaster Canal which terminated at Haigh in 1799, the company having run out of money to continue along a proposed route to Westhoughton to link with the Bridgewater Canal. Despite the expense of building the long flight of locks into Wigan, using the existing Lancaster Canal between Johnson's Hillock and Haigh was a cheaper solution than building an entirely new line. This section south of Johnson's Hillock was leased from the Lancaster Canal Company before being formally taken over by the Leeds-Liverpool Canal Company in 1864.

Extensive industrial activity on the hillside alongside the locks, including a colliery, coke and iron works, has long since vanished and the canal has now been carefully landscaped.

THE ROUTE

Going under both railway and road bridges, the canal now starts its steep ascent through the Wigan flight of locks (the steepest climb on the entire canal), passing long rows of brick terraced housing, so typical of Lancashire colliery towns, and the views getting more impressive as you ascend.

HAIGH COUNTRY PARK occupies the beautiful parkland of Haigh Hall, home of the Bradshaigh and Lindsay families. It was Sir William de Bradshaigh's wife, Lady Mabel, who suffered the sad misfortune during the 14th century of assuming her husband, who had been away for seven years on Crusade in the Holy Land, had been killed in battle. She remarried; unfortunately for her and her new partner, Sir William returned very much alive and without waiting for explanations killed Mabel's new husband. Lady Mabel did penance for her bigamy by having to walk, barefoot and dressed in sackcloth and carrying a candle, once a week to a wayside cross on the outskirts of Wigan. Known as 'Mab's Cross', it still survives, but has been re-erected in Standishgate in central Wigan. William and Mabel lie together, presumably reconciled, under decorated tombs in Wigan parish church. The Hall was rebuilt as a fine neo-classical mansion in the late 18th century when the estate came into the ownership of the Earls of Crawford and Balcarres who made their fortune from local ironworks and the mining of cannel, a hard form of coal which burned brightly and without smoke. Cannel was also used for the carving of decorative objects.

The 260-acre (105ha) estate is now a popular and delightful country park owned and managed by Wigan Metropolitan Borough Council with over 40 miles (64km) of woodland walks, picnic areas, a butterfly safari, a children's zoo and a golf course. The mansion is used for a variety of private and public functions.

Golf Course

Haigh Hall Country Park - once the estate belonging to Haigh Hall and now an amenity run by the Borough Council

THE ROUTE

From this point the canal bears north-westwards along what was originally the southern section of the Lancaster Canal and is once again a level stretch of waterway. Keep directly ahead through much more open countryside of small beechwoods and fields, soon passing areas of attractive woodland on both sides of the canal which follows a narrow shelf along the hillside with Haigh Hall Country Park to the right.

Worthington
Lakes

B5239

A6016

①

STANDISH IS A medieval town which once boasted an important market. It retains many links with its past – medieval stocks, a dipping well, a market cross and an especially fine church, St Wilfrid's. This was rebuilt in Tudor times with classical columns in the nave and an impressive oak roof. There are some richly decorated tombs of the Standishes, Lords of the Manor of nearby Duxbury since the 12th century, who have their own chapel.

The twin lakes in the bottom of the valley north of Standish are known as Worthington Lakes and are popular for angling.

THE ROUTE

Beyond the golf course the land to the left slopes down to the northern outskirts of Wigan and the Douglas valley; the village of Standish is away to the north-west and the electrified west coast main line railway between Euston and Glasgow shares the valley with the main road to Preston.

The canal goes under two bridges carrying farm access tracks and public paths before bearing north-eastwards under the B5239 (1) and crossing over a disused railway line near Red Rock. The next overbridge by the golf course (2) marks the boundary between Greater Manchester and Lancashire. This is a particularly attractive section of the canal.

The bridge at Red Rock, not far from the county border between Greater Manchester and Lancashire

Adlington Hall Farm, south-west of Adlington

A SMALL FORMER cotton-weaving and colliery town alongside the canal, Adlington became a prosperous centre for printing and dyeing of cotton thanks to the purity of local spring water. The village has excellent road and rail access from a wide area, and is now a popular boating centre dominated by the White Bear Marina. There are shops, pubs and a café. There is also a handsome Victorian church with some rich carvings and stained-glass windows executed by the pre-Raphaelite artist Burne-Jones.

It is a relatively short walk of about 2½ miles (4km) to the other side of the M61 to Rivington Reservoir and Lever Park, an extensive area of woodland and moorland walks, hillside gardens and two magnificent medieval tithe barns which are now cafés.

Rivington Pike, site of an an ancient beacon and 1,119ft above sea level, is a notable West Pennine landmark, visible for miles around and a thrilling viewpoint. The estate was given to Bolton Corporation by Lord Leverhulme, the Lancashire soap magnate, and remains one of Lancashire's most popular open spaces and countryside areas.

THE ROUTE

For a time, canal, towpath and River Douglas are once again in close proximity as the canal continues northwards before crossing the river and passing the outskirts of Adlington (train services to Bolton and Manchester). A curve along the contours brings the canal alongside the A6 and the Manchester-Bolton-Blackpool railway line towards Heath Charnock.

A 6

ADLINGTON

Adlington

ouglas

N

DUXBURY HALL, home of the Standish family, was demolished in 1952 and the park to the east of the canal is now the site of a municipal golf course developed by Chorley Council. The area to the south of the park contained a colliery, Duxbury Pit, which, during the Great Depression of the 1920s, was bought out by a group of local unemployed miners who had pooled their savings and borrowed money from the local British Legion. Despite the proximity of roads and railway, this area of the canal keeps its charm. Nearer Chorley there is a particularly attractive area of unspoiled canalside woodland with beech, hawthorne, oak, sycamore, ash, willow, elder and birch.

THE ROUTE

The canal goes through Heath Charnock, which also has a marina, before following the A6 – the former main road to Scotland – going under the A6 and squeezing its way between railway and road before heading past more woodland and into the outskirts of Chorley.

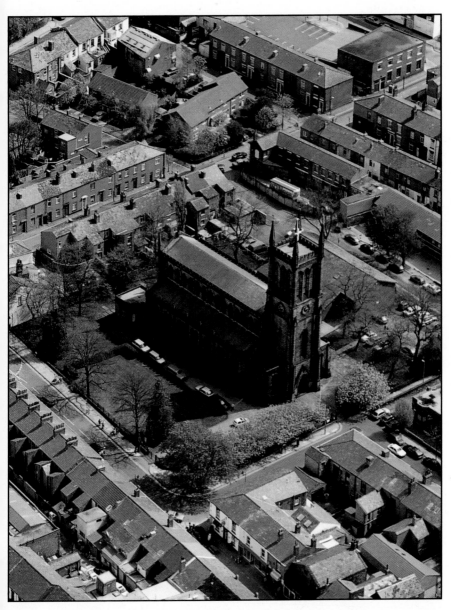

Chorley, birthplace of Henry Tate, founder of the sugar firm and London's Tate Gallery

Chorley to Blackburn

14½ miles (23km)

Breakpoint: Cherry Tree

This section begins somewhat inauspiciously in an area on the outskirts of Chorley, but once away from the motorway interchanges it soon leaves the former Lancaster Canal at Johnson's Hillock and heads north-eastwards through quieter countryside. This is a surprisingly attractive and rural part of central Lancashire, an undulating landscape with the canal taking a meandering route between the high West Pennine moors to the south and the summits of the Forest of Bowland to the north.

Getting to Chorley

Frequent local trains on the Manchester-Bolton-Preston-Blackpool service serve Chorley, Sunday included. Motorists are advised to park either at Preston or Bolton and to catch a train to Chorley to take advantage of direct return trains from Blackburn to their car rather than leaving a vehicle at Chorley.

CHORLEY ENJOYS AN excellent reputation for its lively markets which date back at least to 1498. The covered market is open for business on Tuesdays, Friday and Saturdays, whilst the popular open or 'Flat Iron' market is held on Tuesday. There is a handsome Victorian town hall, and some attractive public buildings in and around the pedestriansed city centre. Astley Park, close to the town centre, includes 150 acres (60ha) of parkland and woodland. There are walks with footbridges over the little River Chor, a children's playground, pets' corner and a nature trail. The house, though rebuilt many times, dates from 1580 and was the home of the Charnock family before being donated to Chorley Corporation after World War I. It is now the town's art gallery and museum, boasting a four-poster bed supposedly occupied by Cromwell after the Battle of Preston in 1648.

THE ROUTE

Keep ahead into Chorley under another overbridge by mills at Cowling, the canal now getting very close to the M61 which skirts the town. As the canal bends left go under another overbridge. (To reach Chorley Station, where a narrow concrete and metal footbridge crosses the canal close to Eaves Lane Hospital (A). Local trains from Chorley operate to Bolton and Preston. If you have decided to return to Wigan for a parked car, catch any train to Bolton and change on to the Southport line to return to Wigan Wallgate.

Astley Park, at the north-west end of Chorley, is a welcome green space in this urban area

Johnson's
Hillock
Locks

Lancaster Canal

M61

B6229

A67

IN FACT THE Leeds-Liverpool Canal didn't really serve the centre of Chorley. The Canal Company's offices and main wharves were at Knowsley, over a mile from the town centre in an area locally known as Botany Bay, and only accessible up the steep hill still known as Botany Brow.

The name Botany Bay was often used in the last century for districts at the edge of a town considered isolated by their inhabitants, so that to live there was like being 'sent to Botany Bay' in Australia. The name probably dates from the time when the area was still considered some distance from Chorley. The M61 has severed the old canalside area from the town, and a new road bridge carries the B6228 over both M61 and canal. The boatyard is now the home of Boatel Cruises and is used for boat hire, canal excursions and the base for a restaurant boat. The Railway Inn provides both meals and liquid refreshment.

Johnson's Hillock flight of seven locks raises the level of the Leeds-Liverpool Canal some 65ft to 363ft above sea level. At the foot of the locks is the point where the Lancaster Canal and the Leeds-Liverpool Canal were joined by the locks. From here the Lancaster Canal headed northwards for a further 3 miles (4.8) to Walton Summit, south of Preston, from where a 5-mile (8km) long horse tramway across the Ribble carried goods which then had to be transferred from boats to tram waggons and back to barges on the northern section of the Lancaster Canal, a time consuming process which ceased when the tramway closed in 1857. A concrete replica of the wooden tressel bridge of the tramway which linked the two sections of the canal now carries a public footpath. Sadly, the M61 was built over the remaining stub of the Lancaster Canal ensuring it could never reopen, though remnants, including surviving fragments of tunnel, can still be seen at Whittle-le-Woods.

Immediately below Johnson's Hillock Locks are Whittle Springs. Spa waters were discovered here in 1840. A hotel, now the Howard Arms, was built for those seeking to enjoy the curative powers of the water. The area became a pleasure park in the late 19th century, a destination for spruced-up coal barges carrying trippers from Chorley and Wigan on popular weekend excursions. The springs also provided water for a local brewery, Whittle Springs Brewery, later taken over by Blackburn brewers Matthew Brown.

THE ROUTE

The towpath continues under the A674 road tunnel into an area dominated by the visual impact and noise of roads. But once under the B6229 things begin to improve as you climb up the impressive series of locks at Johnson's Hillock, past the old junction with the Lancaster Canal near Whittle-le-Woods. You now enter a delightful rural area as the canal bears north-eastwards through seven locks to the top lock and the well-named and positioned Top Lock pub.

WITHNELL FOLD IS a fine example of an early Victorian mill village. It dates from 1843 when a mill on the canal was built there by the Parke family. Later it was taken over by Wiggins Teape and until relatively recently produced high-quality paper used for bank notes. The stone mill, with its square chimney, survives. Thanks to Lancashire Enterprise, there are now several small industrial units being developed here, and new houses are being built to join the 35 mill workers' terraced houses. There is a small park and village chapel and school, as well as village stocks to be seen at the east end of the square. A long cobbled lane links the community with the main Blackburn-Chorley road.

Withnell Fold Nature Reserve has been developed on what was originally a series of filter beds and sludge lagoons built to deal with the outflow from the paper mill on the opposite side of the canal. Disused and derelict for many years, the site was gradually reclaimed by nature. The lagoons and filter beds have become infilled with silt and reed swamp, while further north the former waste tip is overgrown with shrubs. There is public access along waymarked paths.

THE ROUTE

From the Top Lock by Lower Copthurst the countryside opens out, the canal and towpath taking advantage of a shallow valley below Wheelton. Attractive strands of woodland on the hillside to the left provide welcome patches of green after the concrete of motorways. This is a quiet, secluded valley, the canal going under a series of overbridges linking fields on either side. Keep ahead to reach Withnell Fold.

Withnell Fold Nature Reserve, reclaimed industrial land that was associated with the paper mill on the other side of the canal

WITHNELL
FOLD

Nature
Reserve

WHEELTON

A 674

Set some 700ft above sea level, views from the grounds of Hoghton Hall extend across to the Lake District

THE ROUTE

The canal passes below Withnell Fold industrial hamlet on the right, accessible by bridge, and the nature reserve on the left. From here canal and towpath head due north-east in an almost straight line, again crossing bridges. The valley broadens slightly and scattered woodland gives the landscape a more rural feel. Keep the same direction until reaching the crossing under the A675 near Riley Green, past Finnington's marina and boatyard.

AT RILEY GREEN a small marina, boat museum and boatyard thrive alongside a pub and restaurant, Finnington's, which opens all day at weekends. A walk along the A675 leads to Riley Green itself, a small settlement around the crossroads with a pub. There are several attractive waymarked walks in this area, including a path which leads to Hoghton Tower.

One of Lancashire's most famous country houses, Hoghton Tower has its place in English folklore as the place where, in 1617, King James I was so delighted with a joint of beef loin served to his table that he knighted it as 'sirloin'.

A magnificent Elizabethan country mansion in extensive landscaped grounds, it dates back to the 1560s when it was built for Sir Richard Hoghton, Sheriff of Lancashire, and the house remains in the ownership of the de Hoghton family. Hoghton Tower is open to visitors at weekends in the summer and rooms on view include state apartments and the banqueting hall, as well as a unique collection of Chinese dolls' teaware and historic manuscripts. There are gardens and a tea room.

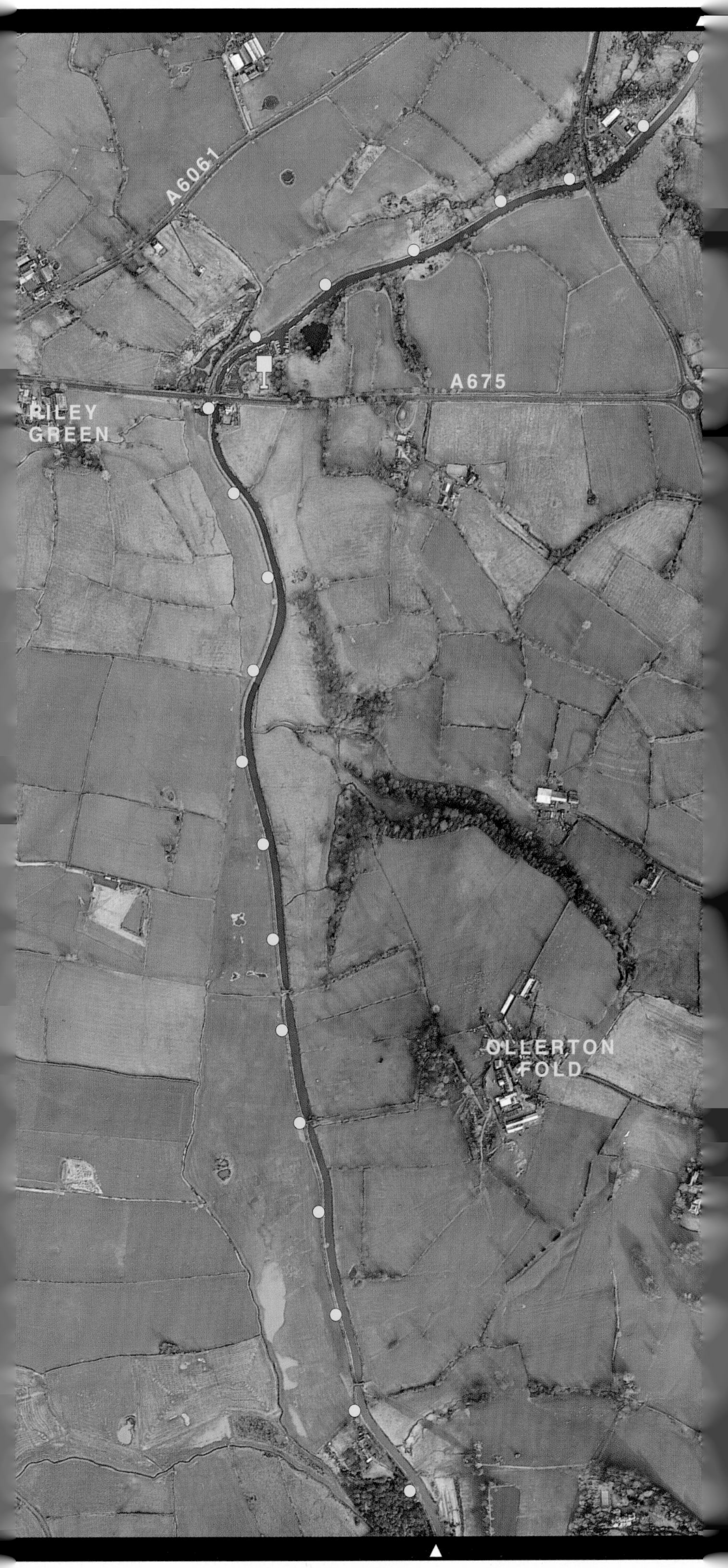
A6061
A675
RILEY GREEN
OLLERTON FOLD

ANOTHER IMPORTANT industrial hamlet, now incorporated in the outskirts of Blackburn, Feniscowles is noted for its Sun paper mill. One of the country's major users of recycled fibre, it turns waste paper into corrugated cases for industrial packing. In times past, coal was delivered by canal to the factories at Feniscowles and the wharfs can still be seen, as well as old canalside warehouses.

A 14-acre (5ha) nature reserve, including a walled garden, has been created at Peasington Old Hall at Feniscowles. Various natural habitats have been established to cater for a wide variety of butterfly species, as well as birds such as nuthatches and lesser-spotted woodpeckers and various small mammals.

THE ROUTE

From Riley Green the canal now bears steadily eastwards, under the A674. Soon industry begins to be more evident, especially on reaching the paper mills at Feniscowles. Pass old wharfs and a long embankment above which the canal swings in a huge U-shaped curve as it crosses the River Roddlesworth (1) and turns northwards to enter Feniscowles. Keep ahead past residential development towards Cherry Tree.

N

A674

FENISCOWLES

Paper
Mill

①

IT'S ONLY A SHORT walk along the main road from Cherry Tree Station to Witton Park – a country park with extensive woods and a nature reserve. There are areas of open parkland, playing fields, riverside areas and a Visitor Centre. The Visitor Centre has exhibition areas, a natural history room, stables, horse-drawn machinery and carriages. There is also a café and toilets.

The borough of Blackburn, with a population of 140,000, is the largest intermediate settlement along the Leeds-Liverpool Canal, and a town to which the canal has contributed a great deal over the last two centuries.

Towards the end of last century, three-quarters of the working population of the town were employed by the textile industry, mainly cotton-spinning and weaving. Now the town has diversified considerably, with engineering still providing the largest single source of employment but followed by industries such as chemicals, plastics, paints, paper-making, electronics and brewing.

Blackburn has been subject to much development in recent years, with its tall Civic Centre tower block dominating the town centre and contrasting with the Victorian town hall and many of the older buildings around such pedestrianised areas as New Market Street. As a major regional centre, Blackburn has its pedestrianised shopping precincts and department stores, and a impressive cathedral dating from 1820-26 which, although largely Gothic in style has both Georgian and modern features, including the powerful sculpture 'Christ the Worker' in aluminium and iron by John Hayward.

Also worth seeing is the Blackburn Museum and Art Gallery in Museum Street whose priceless collections reflect the town's wealth in the past and the generosity of former benefactors – medieval illuminated manuscripts, Japanese prints, a huge collection of English, Greek and Roman coins and watercolours as well as a fine collection of Victorian genre oil paintings, social history sections, and the East Lancashire Regimental Museum. The nearby Lewis Textile Museum in Exchange Street illustrates the contribution to the Industrial Revolution made by great Lancashire engineers and inventors in the textile industry – Kay, Arkwright, Crompton and Hargreaves. The museum has examples and replicas of pioneering looms and textile machinery.

BLACKBURN

THE ROUTE

The canal continues through Cherry Tree, passing houses, warehouses and mills. (For Cherry Tree Station – services to Preston and Blackburn – join the lane from the towpath at Cherry Tree Machines (A) through a gap on the left.) Keep on the towpath as it curves before bearing east through the extensive suburbs and industrial areas of Blackburn, with tower blocks, chimneys and lines of terraced housing up the hillside dominating the view.

The canal crosses over the B6447 and under the railway line from Bolton and Manchester before passing the densely populated streets of Blackburn.

A flight of six locks have to be negotiated through Blackburn

Blackburn to Burnley Barracks

15 miles (24km)

Breakpoints: Church, Hopton

Apart from the Liverpool-Bootle area, this is perhaps the section most heavily dominated by industry, power stations, pylons, workshops and factories, motorways and railway.
There is, however, compensation in some fine views northwards across towards the hills of Bowland and Pendle, and southwards to the West Pennine moors.

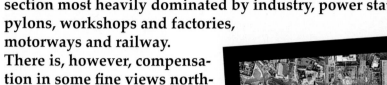

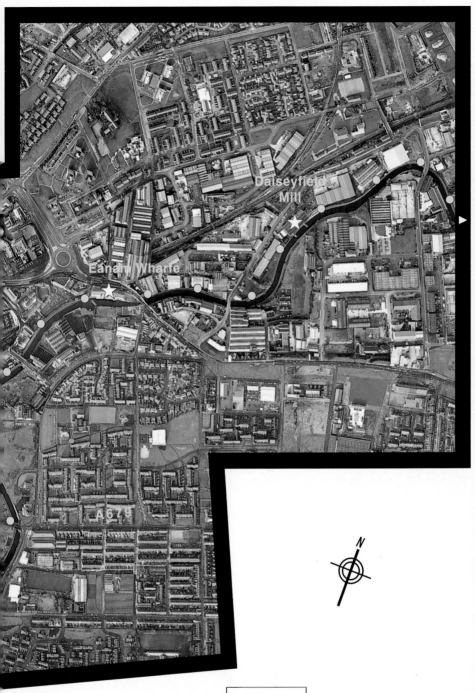

Daiseyfield Mill

Eanam Wharf

A679

N

Getting to Blackburn

Frequent trains operate along the East Lancashire line between Colne, Blackburn and Preston and also direct to Blackburn on the West Pennine Line from Stockport, Manchester and Bolton (winter Sunday services limited from Manchester).

Car users should park at Blackburn (parking space at Eanam Wharf) and return from Burnley by train.

THE ROUTE

Keep ahead up a series of locks (1) past the Nova Scotia Mills before reaching the warehouse with its huge overhang at Eanam Wharf in the centre of Blackburn. A milepost in the warehouse indicates the mileage from Liverpool, 57 (91km) – and the distance to Leeds, 70 (112km).

(A sign just before Eanam Warf indicates the way into the town centre and Blackburn Station.)

EANAM WHARF, built in 1810, was the control centre for canal traffic between Liverpool and Skipton. Boatmen could feed and water their horses at the extensive stable facilities here. These warehouses were extended as recently as 1955 for the carriage of crated machinery to Liverpool, and bales of raw cotton from Liverpool were another important source of traffic.

The warehouse building with its massive overhanging loading bay and internal iron pillars has been superbly restored and now contains a lively Canal Visitor Centre with displays, an information centre and a themed pub and restaurant, the Wharf. There are also workshops, offices, craft centres and shops. Close by is Thwaites Stables where the dray horses of this celebrated Lancashire real ale brewery can be seen between duties – carrying beer on traditional, colourful drays around the streets of the town. The tall-towered brewery is another landmark in the town.

THE ROUTE

Canal and towpath loop north-west past factories and workshop premises, some of them recently relandscaped. The canal gradually moves out of Blackburn, still in a heavily industrialised landscape, before looping northwards and heading for Whitebirk, the Blackburn boundary, before going under the A6119 Preston road by the huge roundabout that forms the western exit of the M65.

From here the canal heads north, past the site of the former Blackburn power station at Whitebirk (now a large retail park), going under the Preston-Colne railway line and into more open countryside. There are more views across nearby hills as the canal curves north-westwards past larger industrial estates.

Rishton
Reservoir

A678

M65

RISHTON RESERVOIR, situated to the south of the cutting carrying the canal into Rishton, was excavated in 1828 to provide water for the increasing amount of water required for locks on the Lancashire side after the canal had been opened throughout its length in 1816. It is also a popular site for recreation, being used for sailing (the home of the East Lancashire Sailing Club) and fishing. In Victorian times it was also popular for skating, though also the site of tragedy one winter when four young skaters were drowned.

Rishton is another example of a town which grew rapidly after the opening of the canal. Industries which took advantage of cheap bulk transport and so flourished by the canal were cotton, fireclay-goods manufacturing, coal mining and paper manufacture. Most of these industries have now disappeared, though traces, including old wharfs and warehouses, can still be seen. Rishton is now largely residential. The Canal Bridge Café in Rishton by the B6535 bridge is a useful refreshment stop.

THE ROUTE

The canal now swings north-eastwards along a shallow cutting towards the town of Rishton, with Rishton Reservoir away to the right. Tall pylons dominate the skyline, but there are fine views to the hills to the north. Keep ahead past rough pasture and signs of small-scale industry around the outskirts of Rishton before the canal once again changes direction, circles southwards and heads across an impressive aqueduct over the M65 then once again goes under the railway line.

Once a busy industrial town that grew up around cotton mills, Rishton is now mainly residential

WITH A NAME beloved by music hall comedians, the former cotton town of Oswaldtwistle has other claims to fame. It was the home of the Peel family, calico printers whose most illustrious son was Robert Peel. It was Peel who established the British police force – and to this day policemen are known as 'Bobbies'. At Stanhill, on the outskirts of Oswaldtwistle, James Hargreaves developed his remarkable 'Spinning Jenny' which was to revolutionise cotton spinning throughout the world.

Until 1974 Oswaldtwistle was the largest Urban District Council in England. It now forms, with Accrington and other towns, part of Lancashire's Hyndburn District.

At Church, near Church Kirk Bridge by the 15th-century Church of St James, is the exact mid-point on the Leeds-Liverpool Canal – 63⅝ miles (101.6km) exactly either to Leeds or Liverpool.

The towpath changes from the left to the right-hand side of the canal through Church between Kirk Gate Bridge and Enfield Bridge because Lord Petre of nearby Dunkenhalgh Hall – who owned land between Rishton and Church – insisted that the path ran along the far side of the canal to discourage poachers on his estate. A health club and hotel occupy Dunkenhalgh today.

THE ROUTE

The outskirts of Oswaldtwistle now lie ahead as the canal passes Accrington Golf Club, and, following the contours, swings around in yet another loop, this time heading for Church. (An exit from the canal here (A) gives access to Church Station.) Follow the towpath as it turns north for ½ mile before changing sides at the crossing bridge at Church Kirk Bridge (1). The canal now makes another sharp turn to the right around the north of Church, going under the A680 motorway link road and heading under the M65 at Enfield Bridge (2) where the towpath returns to the left bank. The canal then heads north-eastwards, close to main road and motorway with the inevitable roar of fast-moving traffic as it approaches Clayton-le-Moors.

As the canal makes its rather circuitous way from Rishton towards Clayton-le-Moors it intersects twice with the M65

BETWEEN 1792 and 1801, until funds were raised to drive the canal westwards to Blackburn and Chorley, Enfield Bridge at Clayton-le-Moors was the western terminus of the canal from Leeds. This quiet Pennine town has a fine 19th-century church with a particularly beautiful carved font. The Applebys, who built the Daisyfield flour mill at Blackburn, came from Clayton and their first mill was built here. The company owned a fleet of boats to service these mills and their mill at Bootle. The small community of Altham was the home of the boatmen and their families who worked carrying local coal from the nearby collieries to customers along the canal. Moorfield Colliery and Coke Works, situated to the south of the canal (now an industrial estate) and once a dominant and polluting feature on the landscape, suffered a terrible pit accident in 1883 in which 67 men were killed. There are several memorials to the victims in Altham Church.

There are fine views across the Calder to Pendle Hill and surrounding hills from this section of the canal.

THE ROUTE

The canal and towpath skirts the edge of Clayton (a fine wallside mural claiming proximity to the mid-point (1)) before finally emerging into more open countryside, though with the M65 ever closer. Head due east past an attractive wooded ravine south of Altham. The canal now makes yet another loop northwards under the road from Huncoat. The giant cooling towers of Padiham power station dominate the landscape.

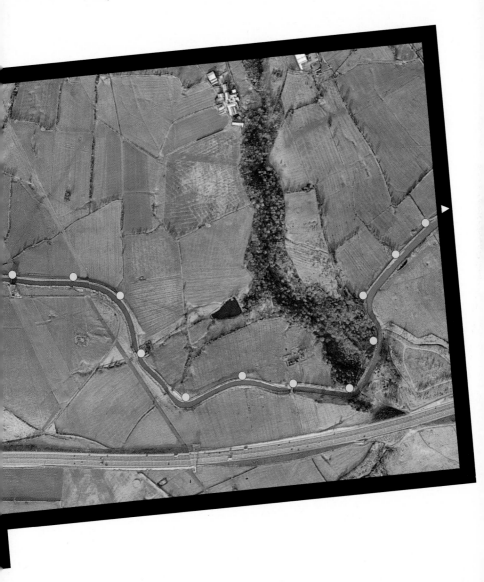

Shuttleworth Hall, a private house just north of the canal to the west of Hapton

HAPTON WAS, until recently, an important centre for coal mining as well as for chemicals. The William Blythe chemical plant along the canal in Church is the only survivor of the many factories which were established alongside the canal to supply local textile printers.

THE ROUTE

Motorway, main road, railway and canal now move together in parallel, the first three taking straight lines, the waterway proceeding in a series of meandering loops which adds to the walkers' distance. At Hapton an exit from the the road crossing at the Bridge pub leads up through the village (A) to the railway station, but most walkers will want to press on to complete the last 3 miles (4.8km) into Burnley.

ANOTHER FORMER colliery town, Padiham has gained in recent years from restoration. Its Victorian buildings and main street winding above the little River Calder give it character, and make it a good vantage point for nearby Pendle. The font in the church is said to have come from Whalley Abbey. Padiham's open-air market takes place on Wednesdays and Fridays.

The late Elizabethan house of Gawthorpe Hall, built around a medieval pele tower, retains its 17th-century character despite being considerably restored last century. It was the home of the Shuttleworths, the most famous of whom was Sir James Shuttleworth, the 19th-century educational reformer. The last member of the family, Rachel Kay-Shuttleworth, was an avid collector of needlework and fabrics, and her collections form the basis of current displays, together with antique furniture and ceramics. Now owned and managed by the National Trust, there are extensive grounds, craft centres and tea shops on the estate.

Burnley's (see page 86) involvement with the textile industry goes back to the Middle Ages. Two years after its market charter of 1294 the town had a fulling

mill, and throughout the Middle Ages and into Tudor times the town flourished as a centre for locally produced wool cloth and other small craft industries. However, it was in the 17th and 18th centuries that the town expanded, its prosperity rooted firmly in its role as a trading centre for the typical Pennine dual economy of hill farming and hand-loom weaving. Many fine yeoman's houses of the period survive in outlying villages. But the Industrial Revolution was to capitalise on this success. The first weaving factory was built on the banks of the River Calder in 1736 whilst the first steam engine was installed in Peel's Mill on Sandygate in 1790. The arrival of the Leeds-Liverpool Canal in 1796 gave a dramatic boost to trade, allowing the importation of bulk supplies of raw cotton to change the town's staple indus-try from the production of wool to the production of cotton. Cotton-spinning and weaving expanded rapidly during the 19th century as Burnley-produced fabrics were exported to India and Africa in great quantities. Only a handful of the town's early mills survive, most being later Victorian and Edwardian mills. One of these, Queen Street Mill, is Europe's last surviving steam-powered mill, and is now, with its original looms and huge mill engine, a remarkable heritage centre

THE ROUTE

The canal continues to follow the M65 before finally looping under both motorway and railway south of the pleasant Pennine town of Padiham. It then heads through Rose Grove, an industrial and residential suburb of Burnely whose charming name belies prosaic reality. About 20 minutes' walk from the bridge that crosses the main A646 (1) lies Gawthorpe Hall, an oasis of peace and beauty.

still producing high-quality cloth. There is a rich architectural heritage of old mills and warehouses, and an impressive, partially pedestrianised town centre which boasts some fine public buildings that bear witness to Burnley's years of prosperity.

Between Mitre Bridge and Finsley Gate the canal goes through a deep canyon between tall stone mill buildings and wharfs, the Weavers' Triangle. This group of buildings forms one of the most remarkable areas of 19th-century industrial heritage in the United Kingdom – weaving and spinning mills, warehouses, foundries, workers' terraced cottages and a fine canopied loading wharf. The former canal toll offices in Manchester Road now form the Weavers' Triangle Visitor Centre with exhibitions and displays, including toys, models and a Victorian schoolroom. An industrial and architectural trail leads along the canal and into adjacent streets.

Gawthorpe Hall, restored by Sir Charles Barry in the 1850s

Burnley Barracks to Colne

10 miles (17km)

Breakpoint: Brierfield

This is the shortest section of the walk from Liverpool to Leeds in terms of distance, but allow time to explore Barrowfield and the excellent Pendle Heritage Centre and perhaps deviate from the canal into the lovely countryside of Pendle.

THE ROUTE

Keep ahead to where the canal works its way through an immense, and in its way impressive, if noisy, spaghetti junction of railway, motorway and trunk road.

The towpath leaves the canal where it enters the Gannow Tunnel on the outskirts of Burnley. At the tunnel entrance leave by the path left (1), turn left at the top, go under two underpasses beneath the main road, and then turn right to go under the roundabout. From the roundabout take the second exit which is signed to Padiham Road and ascend up to the top of the steps. Go straight ahead over the brow of the hill, then straight across the recreation ground, following the path down. Straight opposite are white gates fronting a series of steps which lead down to the tunnel exit. Turn left along the towpath

and keep ahead on another aqueduct over the motorway into the outskirts of Burnley.

Steps soon after the railway bridge at Burnley Barracks lead to the main junction of Westgate and Trafalgar Street with Burnley Barracks Station on the right, (and the Mitre Inn on the left) for frequent trains to Blackburn and Preston. Unless you are in a hurry to return to Blackburn, it is worth continuing another ½ mile along the towpath to the Weavers' Triangle on Manchester Road. From here it is only a short walk into the centre of Burnley. To reach Manchester Road Station (through trains to Leeds via Halifax and also to Preston) turn left into Manchester Road and walk up to the traffic island on the A56 ahead. Turn right here into Trafalgar Road.

Getting to Burnley Barracks

Frequent trains operate from Blackburn (change from Manchester Victoria or Bolton) to Burnley Barracks. Burnley Manchester Road Station with direct trains from Leeds, Bradford and Halifax is about ten minutes' walk away.

Motorists can either park near Burnley Barracks Station, where there is limited parking or alternatively should park at Colne Station where there is a good car park and take the train to Burnley Barracks, before walking back to the car.

Townley Park

Burnley Central

Burnley Embankment

Wharf Museum

Brierfield

BBIERFIELD

①

Pendle
Way

Townley Park, now housing Burnley's museum and art gallery

THE ROUTE

Continue by canal, railway line and urban housing northwards before the canal loops underneath the railway, passing a school, and finally emerging into more open countryside. Pendle Water, a tributary of the Calder, twists through its shallow valley below with the M65 alongside. Pass mills, factories, workshops and more residential areas at Reedley to the west.

(At Brierfield, where the B6248 crosses the canal (1), a gap gives access to the road – turn right past the appropriately named Leeds-Liverpool pub for Brierfield Station by the level crossing.)

Continue past the Smith & Nephew mills, the canal now squeezing past the M65 and its busy junction 12 interchange.

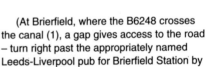

BURNLEY EMBANKMENT, some ¾ mile long (despite being known locally as the 'Straight Mile') and 60ft high, crosses the Calder and forms, with the railway viaduct, a major feature in Burnley. A shorter embankment carries the canal over the River Brun, the source of Burnley's name. The canal passes Thompsons Park with its boating lake to the west and Queen Parks beyond the A6114 to the east. About a mile from the centre of Burnley and the canal towpath is Townley Park. The house itself, ancestral home of the Townley family of Burnley, is an astonishing architectural mix from the 16th, 17th, 18th and 19th centuries. It now houses Burnley's art treasures in an extensive art gallery and museum, as well having arts events and an entertainment centre in the nearby former Mechanics Institute. The parkland and gardens are open to the public daily.

A mainly industrial and residential town, Brierfield still has some handsome mills. At Greenhead Farm, in nearby Reedley, lived Old Chattox, reputedly one of the Lancashire Witches.

Pendle Hill is a celebrated local landmark and forms a focal point for the entire area. From the summit there are glorious views; a popular walk starts from the picturesque village of Barley. The area around Pendle is steeped in legend and history. The villages on its flanks such as Barley and Roughlee contained the homes of the so-called Lancashire Witches, many of whom, including Alice Nutter of Roughlee Hall, suffered persecution, trial and eventual execution at Lancaster Castle in 1612. Though the stuff of romantic legend and colourful fiction, their tragic history is a shameful part of English history.

THE BUSY MANUFACTURING town of Nelson has retained in strong cotton-spinning and weaving traditions, through it has diversified into light industry. Originally known as Marsden from the two small farming and wool weaving settlements of Great and Little Marsden, its name was changed by the Lancashire and Yorkshire Railway to avoid confusion with Marsden in the West Riding of Yorkshire. Nelson now has a partly pedestrianised town centre and a covered modern shopping precinct with a choice of cafés and pubs for refreshment. There are frequent train services from here back to Burnley.

The distinctive, table-top summit of Pendle Hill,
seen here from a northerly direction

THE ROUTE

There is a continuing contrast of industry on the right bank with an open rural landscape beyond the motorway to the left. As the canal enters Little Marsden it passes by a succession of engineering factories, weaving sheds and upholstery works.

Canal and towpath make their way in a series of meanders below Nelson with its mills, weaving sheds and grids of compact terraced housing. Once again the canal must squeeze past a major road interchange at junction 13 before curving around the north of Nelson.

PENDLE HERITAGE CENTRE is housed in a group of 17th- and 18th-century farm buildings. The main farmhouse was the home of the Bannister family whose most famous member was athlete and doctor Roger Bannister, the first man in the world to run a mile in less than four minutes. The Centre has exhibitions, audio-visual presentations and displays about the local and natural history of the area, including balanced accounts of the Pendle Witches and material about local wildlife, local architecture and the area's farming and textile history. An 18th-century garden has been recreated with old-fashioned flowers and vegetables.

The Pendle Way is a 42-mile (67km) long medium distance recreational path around the Borough of Pendle which starts and finishes at the Pendle Heritage Centre. The route, waymarked with a white Pendle Witch logo, is divided into eight short stages, all of around 5-7 miles (8-11km), each of which is described in a leaflet. These are available from the Pendle Heritage Centre of from any Tourist Information Centre in Pendle.

Barrowford, occupying a delightful site on the sheltered foothills of Pendle Hill and alongside Pendle Water which runs through the village, is particularly rich in architectual heritage, with 17th-century handloom weavers' cottages, small early industrial mills and old farmhouses. The entire area offers wonderful opportunities for walks, with a choice of waymarked paths and self-guided trails. Leaflets and guidebooks are available from Pendle Heritage Centre.

THE ROUTE

The canal crosses Colne Water at Swinden Aqueduct and goes underneath the motorway to enter a much more rural landscape, with Barrowford Reservoir on the right.

Canal and towpath now ascend the flight of seven Barrowford Locks into the summit pound of the canal – a stretch of level water 487ft above sea level, extending some 6 miles (9.6km) to Greenber Lock beyond Barnoldswick. Footbridges over the canal and waymarked paths from part-way up the the locks lead to Higherford, an attractive hamlet with weavers' cottages and old farms, forming part of Barrowford. Turn left along the main road (A) to Pendle Heritage Centre. Return by the same route to the towpath and continue to the top of the locks, past Barrowford Lock House and along the summit pound, through delightful rolling countryside to the entrance to Foulridge Tunnel.

Pendle Hill with Windy Harbour Farm, to the north of Barley, in the foreground

Colne to Gargrave

14 miles (23km)

Breakpoint: Barnoldswick

From Foulridge to Leeds it is literally downhill all the way, from the 6-mile (9.6km) long summit pound in the Pennines to the Leeds Basin on the River Aire.

By common consent this is one of the finest sections of the whole canal, most of it deeply rural and fringing the spectacular limestone country of the Yorkshire Dales.

THE ROUTE

(To get to Colne railway station from Foulridge Tunnel follow the old trackbed of the Colne-Skipton railway. From the towpath at the tunnel entrance bear right to join the track which goes over the bridge then turn sharp right on to the grassy trackbed (A). This is an informal path, and an alternative right of way runs from the lane just beyond Blakey Hall Farm to join the old railway near Colne.

For obvious reasons, it is impossible to walk through the tunnel, so this suggested deviation provides an attractive link. Keep in the same direction over the canal to a junction. Turn right here in the lane to where the old railway crosses the lane. Take the second track left (the first being the old railway trackbed), waymarked with a white Pendle Way witch. This leads to the lane opposite Burwain Sailing centre. Turn left, but immediately bear right into the Sailing Centre up the slope towards and past the Sailing Club buildings where the

public path and the Pendle Way follow the embankment round Foulridge Reservoir. Continue to where a signposted path goes over a stile and along a narrow, enclosed way past gardens. Follow this up into a housing estate where it joins a road. Follow the road to Crofts Mill in Foulridge. Turn left by the Hanging Gate pub and continue down Warehouse Lane to Foulridge Wharf. Turn right into the canal basin and small marina, heading past the warehouse and along the towpath once again.

LIKE NELSON, Colne owes its origin as an industrial centre to the Pennine wool trade. It boasts a market charter going back to the 13th century, and had an important Cloth Hall (sadly demolished in 1952) where pieces of finished cloth from outlying weaving villages and farms were bought and sold, with merchants coming form as far as Halifax or Leeds to purchase quality woven and finished cloth. The Market Cross, dating back to 1296, now stands outside the new Market Hall. Colne also has the unique British in India Museum in Sun Street, with a fascinating collection of memorabilia about imperial history in the sub-continent – uniforms, weapons,

A56

FOULRIDGE

Foulridge Reservoir

Disused Railway

documents, photographs and a working model of the Kilma-Simla railway. There is also a small Heritage Centre, managed by Pendle Heritage Centre, in the old Grammar School in the town centre.

Getting to Colne
Regular trains from Preston, Blackburn (connections from Manchester), Rose Grove (connections from Leeds) serve Colne Station.

Motorists are advised to park in Skipton and take the Pennine Motors service through to Colne Station (two bus stops past Colne Bus Stop), returning to Skipton from Gargrave by train or bus.

SALTERFORTH

B6383

NEAR MILL HILL BRIDGE, a stream, County Brook, flows into the canal from Whitemoor Reservoir. Its name indicates that it ran along the pre-1974 county boundary between Lancashire and the West Riding of Yorkshire. The name 'Salterforth' suggests a ford on a medieval salt way; several such fords existed on routes from the salt mines of Cheshire to markets in Yorkshire and the north-east of England. There is a canalside pub, a small marina and an attractive village, past winner of the Best Kept Village in Lancashire award.

It's about a mile from Salterforth to Earby, where, in the 17th-century former Grammar School, you will find the Yorkshire Dales Mining Museum – a remarkable collection of artefacts, tools, photographs and models relating to the history of lead mining in the Yorkshire Dales.

THE ROUTE

Canal and towpath now keep almost due north, towards Salterforth, cutting into and along a gently sloping hillside with fresh green pastures on the left, lower meadows drained by streams to the right, small bridges crossing the waterway, and distant views of the hills ahead. The canal now skirts the village of Salterforth, passes the Anchor Inn, a welcoming canalside pub, goes under the bridge carrying the lane to Park Close, then passes under the B6383 to Barnoldswick.

The terraced houses and narrow streets of Salterforth are typical of this upland area

BARNOLDSWICK, A TYPICAL small Pennine town, has kept much of its character as a mill town, despite expansion in recent years, mainly because of the Rolls Royce Aerospace factory which manufactures jet engines and related technology for the world market. Pronounced Barlick, Barnoldswick has a pleasant centre with shops, pubs and cafés, and good bus services to Skipton and Burnley. At Lower Park Marina, on the canal, there is a canal craft shop and boat hire centre.

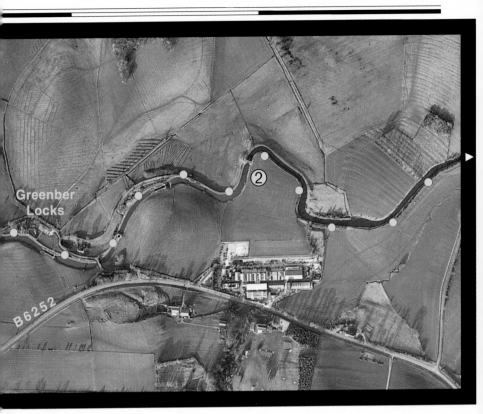

Greenber Locks

②

B6252

THE ROUTE

The canal actually avoids the centre of Barnoldswick, keeping its height along the slopes immediately to the west of the town, but clearly having an influence on its industrial development as mills and larger industrial estates, including the workshops of Rolls Royce Aerospace, are passed. Steps from the second bridge take the B6252 over the canal (1) and are a convenient point from which to leave the canal to walk into Barnoldswick or to catch a bus back to Colne or forward to Skipton.

Beyond the Rolls Royce factories, the path again bends eastwards passing a small picnic site and going down Greenber Locks. For the first time since Church, the towpath changes sides to the right bank at a footbridge (2). The path now swings north, soon crossing the modern boundary into Yorkshire – or more precisely the Craven District of North Yorkshire.

Looking back towards Barnoldswick from the locks north of the town

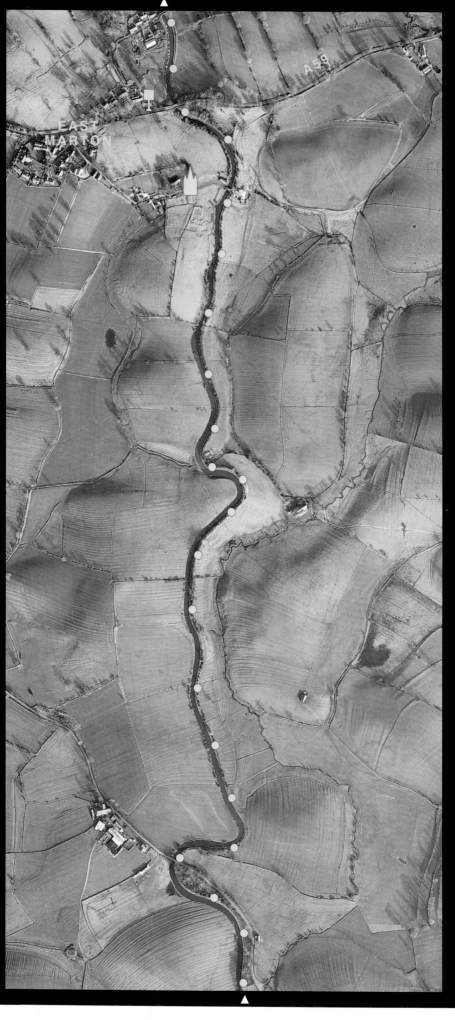

THE PENNINE WAY, Britain's most popular and best known long-distance footpath, or National Trail, runs for 250 miles (400km) between Edale in the Peak District and Kirk Yethom in Scotland over some of the highest summits in the Pennines. The section from East Marton to Gargrave across the Aire Gap is one of the lowest parts of the entire route. A popular 9-mile (14.4km) circular walk is to follow the canal to Gargrave and return by the high-level Pennine Way with its superb views over to Malhamdale and Ribblesdale.

As well as a charming old canalside inn and church with a Norman tower, East Marton has a curious, possibly unique, twin-level, double-arched bridge originally built to carry the Skipton-Gisburn turnpike road over the canal but still carrying the present A59 and its juggernauts, albeit with some recent reinforcement and strengthening. The village also has a shop and café and occasional buses to Skipton. The sharp bends on the canal north of East Marton caused problems in past years with tow-ropes as horses and barges followed the tight curves. A series of posts and rollers was erected on the narrower bends to prevent the tow-ropes from swinging at dangerous angles; most have now vanished. This is a charming, typical lower Dales landscape of rolling hills, scattered beech woods, and fertile pastures enclosed by drystone walls.

THE ROUTE

Once in North Yorkshire, the canal heads steadily north-eastwards, twisting past Copy Hill and between twin green hummocks of Risebrigg Hill, the first of many grassy hillocks or drumlins – glacial waste – that typify this part of Craven around the Aire Gap. After another little meander underneath the lane to West Marton, a long straight stretch of canal through a narrow valley between the drumlins follows. Soon past Langber Barn, the canal is joined by perhaps Britain's most famous long-distance route, the Pennine Way. They continue together to East Marton, with its extraordinary double-arch bridge.

East Marton's secluded little church, at the end of a no-through road, has retained its squat Norman tower

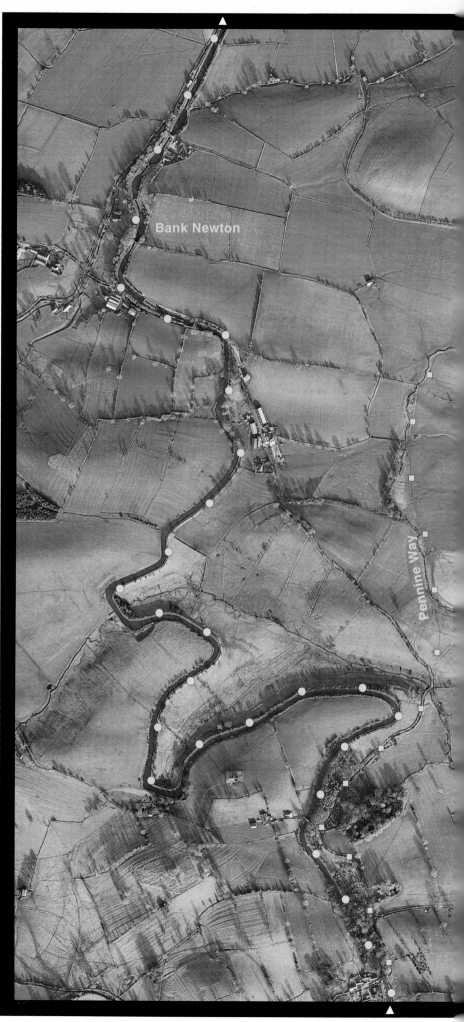

Bank Newton

Pennine Way

The locks (six in all) at Bank Newton, where there is a popular marina and boat-hire centre

THE FORMER CANAL Company's carpenters' yard and workshops at Bank Newton now provide the premises for a marina and one of the largest boat hire centres along the canal. One of the few but doubtless less welcome perks of working for the Canal Company in former years was the provision of a free coffin which was provided for any deceased employee – and made in these workshops.

Nearby Newton Hall, with its long mullioned windows and tall gables dates, from the 17th century. It is a typical Dales yeoman farmer's house of the period.

THE ROUTE

From East Marton the canal enters a narrow, wooded, ravine from which the Pennine Way soon branches away to take a more direct, uphill route to Gargrave. The canal takes the first of a series of serpentine loops to take advantage of the natural contours of the land, winding its way northwards and gradually descending into the Aire Gap, going under Newton Bridge and heading for the locks and crowded marina of Bank Newton. From the basin at the top of the locks there are particularly fine views across to the limestone hills of Craven, with Sharp Haw on Flasby Fell in the foreground.

Gargrave to Steeton & Silsden

13 miles (21km)

Breakpoints: Skipton, Cononley

This section fringes the Yorkshire Dales National Park before following the canal on its way through one of the most important natural passes of the Pennines, the Aire Gap. From its source in Malhamdale, the River Aire flows between the high gritstone moors of the Yorkshire Dales and the South Pennines through a landscape dominated by scores of drumlins formed from the clay and boulders left by retreating glaciers. This relatively low pass, rising to little more than 400ft compared with bleak moorlands of over 1,200ft on either side, has long been a strategic communication link between West Yorkshire and the Cumbrian coast.

Getting to Gargrave

Trains on the Leeds-Skipton-Lancaster line provide a limited but fairly conveniently timed weekday service to Gargrave, also on summer Sundays, but there is no morning service on winter Sundays. Pennine Motors provide a very much more frequent service from Skipton to Gargrave on their Settle/Ingleton/Malham routes, but again no services operate on winter Sunday mornings.

Motorists should either park at Gargrave to return by direct train from Skipton or Steeton & Silsden (winter Sundays included), or leave their car at Skipton going on to Gargrave by bus or train to take advantage of much more frequent Metrotrain Airedale services from Steeton

GARGRAVE EXPANDED expanded in the 18th century as a coaching town on the busy Keighley-Kendal turnpike road but it also enjoyed a period of additional prosperity at the end of the century when it became the western terminus of the Yorkshire section of the canal. The coming of the railways reduced the town's importance, and it is now a quiet Dales community with a long twisting main street. It is a stopping-off point for cyclists heading for the Lake District or higher Dales, and for walkers along the Pennine Way heading for Malham. There is an attractive village green past which bubbles the infant River Aire. The church was rebuilt in 1852, though its fine 15th-century Perpendicular tower was thankfully retained. The station, too, is of interest, having some original pre-Midland 'Little Northwestern' buildings of the later 1840s which so far have escaped demolition.

THE ROUTE

North-west of Bank Newton the towpath crosses to the left bank and for a time joins the parallel narrow lane, before returning back to the right bank as it heads into the Upper Aire valley, with more fine views across to the Yorkshire Dales National Park ahead. The River Aire is crossed at Priestholme Bridge (1), and the canal goes underneath the Leeds-Settle-Carlisle railway, one of Britain's most scenic railways, which now accompanies the waterway all the way to the centre of Leeds. Canal and towpath continue to curve eastwards, down the first of Gargrave's six locks, before going under the busy A65 trunk road and hugging the northern edge of the village past moorings and wharves.

At the next lock and crossing point by Gargrave House turn right into the village centre along West Street into the centre of Gargrave. Here there is a choice of cafés, pubs, shops, accommodation and transport to Skipton. From the centre of the village the lane to Broughton leads over the river and past Gargrave Church to Gargrave Station for trains on the Leeds-Lancaster line to Skipton and Leeds. Sadly this service is not frequent, though well-timed late afternoon and early evening services (Sunday included) will provide for the needs of most walkers. Alternatively, Pennine Motors buses from outside the Dalesman Café will take you into the centre of Skipton.

Sandwiched between the River Aire and the canal, Gargrave is an attractive village much visited by those exploring the National Park

THE ROAD FROM Grassington to Gargrave was built by the Duke of Devonshire in the 1780s specifically to provide good access to the canal from his extensive mines in Upper Wharfedale. Lead ores were mined in deep mines on Grassington and Hebden Moors and smelted at the great Cupola Mill – whose chimney and flue system are still to be seen – then brought by cart to Gargrave for storage. Limestone was also carried from local quarries as was calamine (zince ore) from Malham Moor.

The outflow from Winterburn Reservoir down Eshton Beck is also fed into the canal at this point as a booster supply, the surplus continuing at the far side of the canal into the River Aire. Close to the bridge is a lovely surviving example of a tollbooth on the Keighley-Kendal turnpike road. The new Gargrave bypass could make considerable changes to the landscape at this point.

One of the largest manufacturers in Craven, the international company of Johnson & Johnson, specialising in medical, hygiene and baby-care products, sited its factory in this part of Craven because of the purity and dust-free nature of the air – essential for the manufacture of products where hygiene is of paramount importance.

ROUTE DIRECTIONS

Continue past Grassington Road bridge, with its tall warehouse and wharfs, and Ray Bridge before going over Eshton Beck under the A65 at Holme Bridge by a further set of locks (1). The large, modern factory with a prominent chimney to the right is Johnson & Johnson's of Gargrave. The wooded hillside to the left is Sharp Haw, a popular landmark and viewpoint, forming part of the Flasby Fell group.

The canal now swings south-eastwards, parallel to the A65 and the River Aire, with views over open pastures to the hills beyond. Pass Highgate Swing Bridge (2) as the canal curves back towards the road.

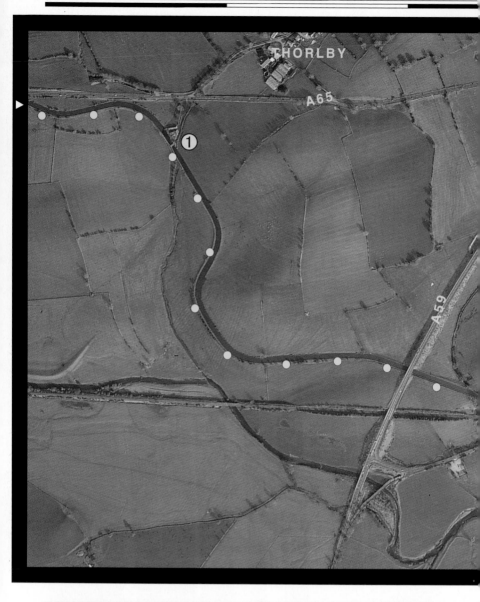

THORLBY

A65

A59

①

Skipton Castle and the parish church stand at the northern end of the town's wide High Street

THE A65 FORMS the southern boundary of the Yorkshire Dales National Park at this point. National Parks in the United Kingdom are neither nationally owned nor are they 'parks' in the usually accepted sense of the word. The National Park is largely privately owned and managed, though with additional protection through planning legislation and special management measures. It is one of 11 such Parks in England and Wales and covers over 680 square miles (1,760 sq km). The Yorkshire Dales are world famous for their outstanding limestone and gritstone moorland scenery, the beauty of the river valleys, and the character of their villages. It is also an area known and loved as walking country of exceptional variety and interest, and for its unrivalled cave and pot-hole systems.

ROUTE DIRECTIONS

Road and canal pass close together by Thorlby Swing Bridge (1) before the canal bears right in a broad curve between the green mounds of drumlins. Hoober Hill is the prominent hillock on the left as the canal swings southwards towards the railway line. The enormous concrete bridge and flyover ahead carries the A59 Preston road, forming the western part of the Skipton bypass. The canal goes underneath, heading into a narrow shelf on the side of Gawber Hill shared by the old A59 road into Skipton and railway. The road crosses the railway and goes parallel to the canal at Niffany Viaduct where for a time the towpath joins the road, before branching off again along the canal into Skipton.

ORIGINALLY A SAXON settlement, in Norman times Skipton was chosen as the site of a powerful Norman castle guarding strategic routes into the Aire Gap from the east. The medieval castle survives and, despite extensive 17th-century rebuilding, is one of the finest examples of a castle of its period (open daily). The pattern of a typical Norman town can still be clearly seen, with the church by the castle at the head of the town and a High Street extending below

THE ROUTE

The canal again meanders, this time under the high concrete shelf carrying the main Skipton bypass heading southwards to Keighley, before the towpath loops back into Skipton, passing gardens, old mills and small streets of ter-raced housing. Pass the viaduct carrying the Carlton Road and the entrance to Aire-ville Park – Skipton Station is almost opposite. Keep ahead with allotments on the left and some fine old mills and wharfs on the right, including the massive former Dewhurst's Sewing Cotton Mill. The canal passes Skipton wharf with its old crane and unloading wharf and warehouses, now part of an outdoor shop and nightclub complex, to reach the main road into Skip-ton at Belmont Bridge. Go up the slope on the right to the road, turning left to the town centre and canalside areas. If you want to explore the Springs Branch (see page 113), it is best reached from the top of the High Street, past the church, where narrow steps on the far side of the canal bridge lead to boat moorings and the towpath along the branch. The towpath continues under Belmont Bridge past more moorings, the car park and bus station, heading through Middle Town and New Town, an area of dense terraced housing, old factories and mills. You soon go under the former Yorkshire Dales Railway line to Swinden Quarry. Closely parallel to the main Keighley road, the canal heads due south.

As the canal makes its way through the middle of Skipton it passes under nine bridges. Few walkers can resist spending time here

both. There are old inns and shops, courtyards and alleyways and a colourful street market (markets are held daily except on Tuesdays and Sundays). Many of the old medieval 'backs' which were converted into workshop areas or crammed with workers' cottages around old courtyards in the Industrial Revolution are now attractive shopping arcades or precincts.

As well as an excellent choice of pubs, cafés, restaurants and shops, places to visit in Skipton include the medieval parish church with its tombs of the famous Clifford family of Craven and Westmorland, and the excellent Craven Museum occupying the top floor of the Victorian town hall. Here there are collections of natural and local history, geology and material relating to the Dales lead-mining industry.

Low Bradley Moor rises up east of the canal south of Low Bradley

THE ROUTE

Snaygill Industrial Estate, with its sewage works, factory units and warehouse, is soon passed, as is the new Randalls Hotel with its lounges and restaurants overlooking the waterside. Road and canal now head south in tandem, then the canal swings away in another long loop, this time going below the old mill town (now a largely residential suburb of Bradley), before returning to the noise of the bus main road. If you plan to cross to Cononley (hourly train service back to Skipton – some through to Gargrave), take the field path (A) opposite where the canal rejoins the main road by a bridge. This crosses to a bend in the river and follows the riverside to Cononley.

THE OLD SPRINGS BRANCH was built in the 1770s through a deep ravine alongside Eller Beck at the back of Skipton Castle to carry limestone to the Bradford and Aire valley ironworks. The crushed stone was brought by rope-hauled tramway from a quarry at Haw Bank, near Embsay, and gravity-fed into waiting barges. The walk along the towpath by Eller Beck behind the high castle walls, past a surviving water-wheel at High Mill, is beautiful and fascinating. It leads to Skipton Woods, an area of woodlands with lakes which are open to the public (afternoons only).

Really two villages, High and Low Bradley, the older part of this hillside village contains some lovely old weavers' cottages and farms, as well as later mills.

Cononley was an important lead-mining village until the later years of last century. Mines high up on the moors produced quantities of lead which were smelted in Cononley Smelt Mill, whose hilltop chimney can be seen from the Aire valley. Long rows of miners' and weavers' cottages survive below the steep hillside, whilst its recently reopened station has attracted a new generation of commuters.

THE TWIN VILLAGES of Farnhill and Kildwick, like Bradley, contain some fine weavers' cottage and 17th- and 18th-century farmhouses, one of which, Kildwick Grange, is now a restaurant. Kildwick in particular enjoys a sheltered, sunny, west- and south-facing hillside position.

The Tudor Kildwick Church, the 'Lang Kirk o' Craven', is of generous dimensions, reflecting the prosperity of the Pennines in that period and the village also has a celebrated ivy-covered pub, the White Lion.

Kildwick Church stands right by the canal at the bottom of the village. Very steep streets lead away from it

THE ROUTE

A stretch of about ¾ mile follows with fine views across the valley on the left. Cononley Chimney is a notable landmark. Go through the edge of Farnhill Wood on the hillside to the left before going under Farnhill Bridge. The canal then makes a long loop, now away from the road, below Farnhill itself (a swing bridge takes paths into the village) before twisting back to Kildwick and passing between the main part of the village and the church. From Kildwick the canal heads due east on a more elevated shelf which gives fine open views across the broad, flat-bottomed Aire valley to the steep hillsides and mill villages of Cross Hills and Sutton in-Craven. The Steeton bypass with its fast-moving traffic seems to fill the valley floor with its noise. However, canal and towpath move away along the hillside, with pastureland on each side of the canal. The large group of buildings on the floor of the valley is Airedale Hospital.

Steeton & Silsden to Shipley

11 miles (17.5km)

Breakpoint: Bingley

**This day's walk goes through Airedale, through what might
be described as classic West Riding country – mills, moors,
stone walls and green valley – which even though blighted
by modern industry and a high-speed road which is to all
intent and purpose a motorway, has the craggy heights of
open moors above to give a sense of space and grandeur. A
number of massive glacial moraines not only give the valley
floor a surprisingly undulating character, but cause the river
to serpentine between low hillocks – unlike the canal which
takes a more direct, elevated route, contouring along the edge
of the hillside.**

Getting to Steeton & Silsden
Frequent MetroTrain services (Airedale
Line) from Leeds, Bradford Forster
Square, Keighley and Skipton serve Sils-
den Station – Sundays included.
Motorists should park at Steeton &
Silsden Station (large free car park) and
return by train.

SILSDEN, ALTHOUGH much expanded
in recent years as modern commuter
estates have spread along the hillsides, is
still a typical stone-built Pennine
town at heart. A stream

with an accompanying chorus of ducks
runs alongside the winding main street,
and there are some attractive 18th- and
19th-century cottages and shops, an
early 18th-century church and Victorian
chapel, a meeting room and cottages, as
well as mill buildings alongside the
canal. A choice of cafés and pubs offer
refreshment.

Warehouses alongside the canal at Silsden indicate the town's industrial past

THE ROUTE

The canal curves past farms and swing bridges towards Silsden, its modern housing developments covering the hillside before the older part of the town, with its wharfs and marina, is reached. Keep ahead to the bridge carrying the A6034 where steps lead up to the village centre to the left.

It's about ¾ mile to Steeton & Silsden Station, though an alternative is to catch a bus (services 712, 762 or 765) from near the canal bridge which will stop on the overpass above Steeton Station or allow you to carry on into Keighley. There are frequent trains (Sundays included) to Keighley, Leeds and Bradford, and back to Skipton or Gargrave.

Alder Carr
Wood

A629

THE STEEP MOORLAND to the north and west of the canal forms the southern flank of Rombalds Moor, a massive area of gritstone and heather moorland and woodland crowned with radio masts that divides Airedale from Wharfedale.

Footpaths lead from the canalside up on to Holden Gate, Rivock Edge and, further afield, past Doubler Stones to Ilkley Moor – all much loved walking country for generations of West Riding people.

THE ROUTE

The canal soon passes Silsden's last housing estate before entering open country. It hugs the hillside on an elevated position above the valley to give good views to the right across the flat, green valley bottom of the River Aire shared by railway and new trunk road to the steep, partially wooded hillsides above Steeton and Uttley. To the left the land rises steeply up sloping pasture past scattered farms.

Pass the swing bridges at Brunthwaite and Holden, the canal now curving round a steep bastion of the moorland above Low Holden Farm, with Alder Carr Wood coming almost to the canalside. Holden Park Golf Course is on the other side.

Cliffe Castle, Keighley, see page 121

THE ROUTE

Now follows a long, straight stretch of canal as it curves to the north of Keighley. The first part is rural in character, with extended woodland fringing the canal to the left, and open views to the right. As Riddlesden is approached, past Leaches' Bridge, housing comes down to the canal edge. Keep ahead to East Riddlesden, where there is an attractive small wharf and warehouse, to Granby Lane and bridge by the Marquis of Granby pub.

Almost directly opposite, across the main

East Riddlesden Hall. A formal walled garden and a monastic fishpond are features of the grounds which run down to the River Aire

road and traffic lights, is the entrance to East Riddlesden Hall.

Keighley town centre is about a mile away, directly down the main road, which can be avoided by catching one of the frequent bus services which operate into the town centre.

EAST RIDDLESDEN HALL is an outstanding example of a 17th-century manor house. In the mid-17th century it was owned by the Murgatroyds, local clothiers and ardent Royalists, who extended the house to its present size. The house, reputedly haunted, is noted for an usual rose window, its beautiful panelled rooms, intricate plasterwork and collections of pewter, domestic utensils and oak furniture. There are formal walled gardens and a monastic fishpond. The 120-ft long Great Barn is one of the best preserved examples of a 17th-century tithe barn in the North of England. It houses a collection of farm carts and agricultural machinery. There is also a tea shop. The house is now owned and managed by the National Trust.

Keighley grew rapidly last century as a centre for both textiles and heavy engineering. Its mainly Victorian town centre has been supplemented by a covered shopping princinct, whilst features to attract the visitor include the splendid Cliffe Castle Museum and Art Gallery in a former wool merchant's mansion, the Yorkshire Car Collection of vintage cars in Grange Street and the Worth Valley steam railway linking Keighley with the Brontë town of Haworth.

EAST MORTON, West Morton and Micklethwaite are typical small Pennine weavers' settlements with some handsome 17th- and early 18th-century yeomen's houses and weavers' cottages. Micklethwaite Mill is now a craft centre – the Micklethwaite Studio Workshop.

The high gritstone crags of Druids' Altar (see following map), were used as the fictional setting for a lurid and illicit meeting of Chartists in Benjamin Disraeli's novel, *Sybil*. Disraeli was a friend of the Ferrands, local landowners and politicians, and stayed with the family at their mansion at St Ives (now an attractive country park) close by.

THE ROUTE

Continue through an area of suburban housing, behind back gardens and, once past Swine Bridge, again enjoying more open countryside to the left. The steep hillside slopes up first towards East and West Morton and then up to Micklethwaite. The elevated position of the canal permits fine views down the Aire valley, the crags on the hillside to the right forming Druids' Altar, a prominent viewpoint.

Micklethwaite, onetime weavers' village. It can easily be reached from the towpath

BINGLEY FIVE RISE and Three Rise Locks bring the water level of the canal down 108ft to 226ft above sea level at Park Bridge.

When the first boat, carrying limestone from Craven, made its slow way down the staircase locks on 21 March 1774, church bells rang out in Bingley. Along the towpath a band started to play and a volley of shots was fired into the air by local soldiers. The locks, designed by John Longbotham, have changed little since they were built and are considered one of the wonders of canal engineering. Passage by boat through the Five Rise Locks takes about half an hour, and at busy period boats have to wait in the basin between the two sets of locks. Going through the Three Rise takes about 20 minutes, requiring a full hour to complete the staircase. The stone building above the footbridge at the top of the Five Rise was originally a staging stable where horses towing barges could be rested or changed. The lock house immediately at the top of the locks was built in the 1880s using the stone from a demolished warehouse in Liverpool which was carried here in stages by barge. In former times there was a carpenter's shop and wooden crane here. There is now a boatyard at the top of the locks.

Three Rise Locks, although dwarfed by their larger neighbour, also make an impressive sight, the mooring areas below the locks often colourful with narrowboats and canal cruises in the summer months. There are extensive views across the town and along Airedale from the top of the locks.

Bingley is one of the oldest towns in Airedale. William Paganell, the Norman founder of the Augustinian priory at Drax, built a church here around 1120, whilst land in the parish was acquired by religious orders, including monks from Rievaulx Abbey, for sheep farming, and iron smelting. After Maurice de Gaunt obtained a market charter from King John in 1212, Bingley developed into a busy market town, with the church and its inn close by and a ford near the present bridge over the river. By Tudor times, prosperous yeoman farmers had already established the clothing trade and the town was linked to the Piece Hall at Halifax by moorland packhorse tracks. Bingley Church was rebuilt in 1518 and the Grammar School, which still flourishes as the local comprehensive, was founded in 1529.

THE ROUTE

From Micklethwaite Bridge it is a short walk to the right (A) down to Crossflatts Railway Station. The route continues southwards into Bingley Gorge past extensive moorings and down Five Rise and Three Rise Locks. Keep ahead alongside the intrusive new road over which there is access to Bingley Railway Station and car park. The towpath continues alongside an impressive group of warehouses and factories through the central part of Bingley.

Bingley Five Rise Locks, a masterpiece of canal engineering. They can only be used under the supervision of the lock keeper

THE ROUTE

Keep ahead to the Fisherman's Inn at Dowley Gap and Dowley Gap Locks (Two Rise). Just beyond the locks the towpath changes sides to the north bank of the canal (1) and crosses a long aqueduct over the shallow River Aire. Continue past Hirst Woods, and Hirst Lock, soon passing the cricket ground on the outskirts of Saltaire.

Shipley Glen (below and right) is a local beauty spot lying north of the canal between Bingley and Shipley

OLD SALT WAYS from Cheshire to medieval fairs at Baildon high on the moors above crossed down to the River Aire at Cottingly Bridge. The Fisherman's Inn, though modernised, is a good example of a canalside pub. Dowley Gap Locks bring the canal down 10ft to 216ft above sea level. Hirst Woods Aqueduct carries the Leeds-Liverpool Canal more than 30ft above the River Aire. It was built by local contractors and stonemasons Jonathon Sykes of Oulton and Joseph Smith of Woodlesford between 1771 and 1773. There are good views across the shallow River Aire – a good place to see dippers in the summer months.

Hirst Woods, relic Pennine oakwoods on a glacial moraine above river and canal, are a rich area for wildlife. An outline of a stone circle can be seen in the centre of the wood. It is reputed to be part of an Iron Age shepherd's dwelling. A bridge at the Saltaire end of the wood gives access from the towpath.

Hirst Woods

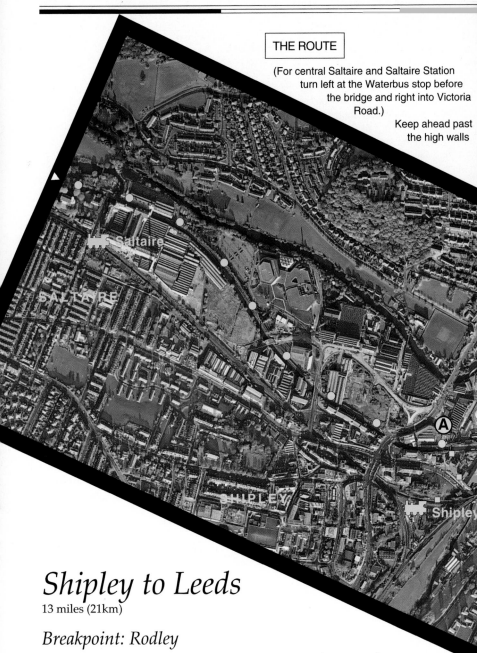

THE ROUTE

(For central Saltaire and Saltaire Station
turn left at the Waterbus stop before
the bridge and right into Victoria
Road.)

Keep ahead past
the high walls

Saltaire

SALTAIRE

SHIPLEY

Shipley

Ⓐ

Shipley to Leeds
13 miles (21km)

Breakpoint: Rodley

**The walk along the canal from Liverpool to Leeds
reaches a fitting conclusion in the Kirkstall valley, a
remarkable wedge of well-wooded countryside which extends
into the very heart of the city of Leeds. It also follows, for part
of its route, the Museum of Leeds Trail through the valley, a
heritage trail which links the Leeds Industrial Museum with
the City Centre mainly along the canal towpath. The trail is
rich in themes which illuminate aspects of the city's history,
ending at Leeds Basin.**

Getting to Shipley.
Frequent MetroTrain services (Airedale
line) from Leeds, Bradford Forster
Square and Keighley. Motorists should
park at Shipley Station (large free car
park) and return by train.

SALTAIRE IS one of the most
remarkable settlements on the whole of
the Leeds-Liverpool Canal. It takes its

name from Sir Titus Salt (1803-1876), the
Bradford wool magnate who made his
fortune from developing a new process
of spinning apalca wool from South
America. Faced in the 1850s with the
problems of a grimy, congested and pol-
luted city centre in Bradford, Titus Salt
moved both factory and workforce out
into what at that time was a greenfield
site along the River Aire and Leeds-

of Salts Mill and its annex, past a small group of early 19th-century canalside cottage on the left and to Shipley Wharf on the right (Apollo Canal Cruisers). Continue under the A6038 main road to a metal pedestrian bridge. Cross the bridge (A) and go along a short alleyway to the main road and the main entrance to Shipley Railway Station for frequent MetroTrain Airedale Line services to Leeds, Bradford, Keighley and Skipton.

Leaving the dock, canal and towpath now follow river and railway north-eastwards, soon going underneath the Bradford-Ilkley branch line, and passing factories, sheds and allotments.

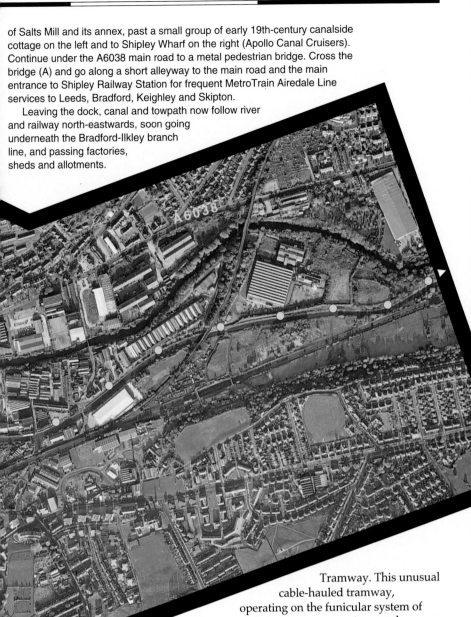

Liverpool Canal. Salt's massive mill is currently being transformed into a major new art gallery which will serve the Bradford region.

Titus Salt did not just create a mill at Saltaire, but an entire 'model' industrial village based on the example of Robert Owen's New Lanark in Scotland. Neat, geometric streets of comfortable terraced houses were laid out, the main street, Victoria Road named after the Queen herself, the second street by the railway after Prince Albert, others after Sir Titus and his wife, Lady Caroline, and their various children.

Less than ten minutes' walk from the canal towpath, at Saltaire, and directly behind Robert's Park, is the Shipley Glen

Tramway. This unusual cable-hauled tramway, operating on the funicular system of two balancing cars evening out the energy requirements, was built in 1887 by Sam Wilson to serve the gardens and pleasure grounds at the top of the glen on the edge of Baildon Moor. In its heyday before World War I, up to 15,000 people a day were carried to this popular Bradford beauty spot which as well as a small funfair, pubs, café and garden centre, includes a typical sandstone Pennine gill covered by oak and birch woods. Close by is the Brackenhall Countryside Centre, a small countryside interpretation and visitor centre.

One of the last commercial operators of traditional narrowboats along the canal, Apollo Canal Cruisers have adapted their boats and their business for the leisure market, and now operate Metro Waterbus along the Leeds-Liverpool Canal during the summer months between Shipley Wharf, Saltaire, Dowley Gap and Bingley, as well as lunchtime and dinner cruises. Local notices give times of services.

SHIPLEY HAS SOME attractive period cottages, probably originally canal workers dwellings, along the towpath. Though the town is surrounded by mills, most of them are no longer devoted to the manufacture of worsted fabric. The parish church on the Keighley road dates from 1823, with some Victorian rebuilding. There are some interesting older houses, including a house dated 1593, in Kirkgate near the church. The main focus of the town is its large, modern market square.

Interesting in its own right is the railway station, a unique, surviving example of a triangle junction station with lines spreading out in four directions to Leeds, Skipton, Bradford and Ilkley, with no less than five platforms situated on different sides of the triangle, the latest opened as

The Nosegay

recently as 1992 to avoid Leeds trains having to share the same tracks with those to Skipton. All the lines are about to be electrified, and platforms 4 and 5 already carry through Inter-City services between Bradford Forster Square and London Kings Cross, the station being developed as an important park-and-ride station for north Bradford. The station buildings themselves, including waiting rooms and high-ceilinged booking hall, are, however, pure Midland Railway in style and character, with only the electric lighting replacing gas as a concession to the Inter-City era.

The deviation around the hillside at Buck Wood follows the longer route along river valley rather than taking the direct line through the tunnel as the later railway does. This was because when it was built in the 1770s canal tunneling was still in its infancy and such engineering works were kept to a minimum, resulting in a longer 'contour' canal to taking advantage of the natural topography of the area.

THE ROUTE

At Buck Wood (A) the railway enters Thackley Tunnel, whilst river and canal skirt north-eastwards in a long curve to avoid the steep hillside which culminates in the hill with the poetic name, The Nosegay. This is a lovely hillside of mixed woodland, mainly oak, with good views up across to Esholt Woods on the hillside ahead.

Esholt, the village familiar to many as the setting for the soap opera Emmerdale

THE ROUTE

Field Lock, taking the canal down another 10ft, is soon passed, and once around the broad curve the canal follows the river valley southwards alongside the extensive Esholt Water Treatment Works. It then rejoins the riverside and goes under the railway as it emerges from Thackley Tunnel by Bottom Farm. The canal, still keeping to the slope of the hillside, now heads for Apperley Bridge, with the river bearing away from the canal to go under Apperley Viaduct carrying the railway. The canal passes the picturesque Dobsons Lock and the British Waterways Office, by the swing bridge, and goes south of Apperley Bridge with its old turnpike-era inn, the George and Dragon, before going under the busy A658. River and canal come together again for a short stretch, the canal maintaining its height along the contour below Calverley Wood, the river swinging north beyond the railway.

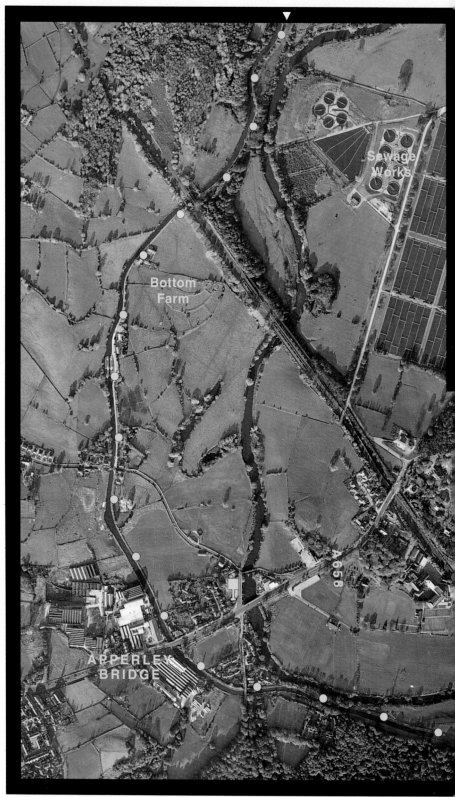

Apperley Bridge

IN THE MIDDLE AGES Esholt was the setting for a nunnery and the compact farm and mill village which grew up around the remains of the nunnery is now well-known as the setting for the popular Yorkshire Television soap opera, *Emmerdale*.

The large works treating industrial and domestic waste from Shipley and north Bradford is so extensive it once had its own internal railway, the engines adapted to burn the oils from waste wool. One of the locomotives is kept in Bradford Industrial Museum at Moorside Mills.

CALVERLEY

N

THE CANAL FOLLOWS an elevated position overlooking the lower Aire valley, with surprisingly rural views across the woods and valley itself. The woods are a mix of beech, alder, sycamore, oak and birch. Calverley church tower makes a notable landmark from the canal in a deceptively rural setting above pastureland and woods.

Once an industrial village on the outskirts of Leeds, Rodley keeps its own identity. It has an attractive main street with stone-built houses, many with mullioned windows. The village developed around the canal in the late 18th century, and there is a small marina and a canalside pub. Rodley was also famous for its crane works, further along. These were established in 1820 and eventually developed into one of the world's leading builders of steam cranes and excavators for railways, canal and civil engineering works throughout the world. Examples of Rodley-made Smith and Booth cranes can be seen in the Leeds Industrial Museum (see page 141).

Calverley Church, on the A657. Most of the village lies to the south of the main road

THE ROUTE

Canal, river and railway continue through a particularly lovely and richly wooded part of central Airedale. Keep ahead to the bridge carrying the Leeds ring road with the Sandos pharmaceutical works near Horsforth. The canal now turns south to Rodley with its boatyard. This is a useful mid-point with a canalside pub and local shops. Frequent buses go from here to central Leeds or back to Shipley. The towpath continues past boatyards and moorings, a swing bridge and engineering yards before curving sharply northwards again with the river towards Newlay Bridge.

A6120

RODLEY

Rodley, see page 134

NEWLAY

WHITECOTE

AT NEWLAY BRIDGE and Bramley Fall Woods an iron bridge dating from 1819 crosses the River Aire. It was built to link the road from Whitecote (the 18th-century house passed on the canalside) to enable John Pollard of Newlay House to have access to the Leeds-Horsforth turnpike road along the valley side above, a toll of a halfpenny being charged for its use. Newlay Bridge forms a focal point for the Kirstall Valley Park, a conservation area of canal, riverside and woodlands through which there is a network of attractive walkways, accessible by bridges across the canal at the two sets of locks. There is a picnic area by the canal and an inn, the Abbey Inn, by the railway. There were once extensive quarries in the woods, millstone grit being quarried and dressed here from the 12th century and used for the construction of Kirkstall Abbey. Kirkstall Forge was probably founded by the Spencer family in the 17th century, utilising water power from the little Hawksworth Beck which flows into the river at this point. By the middle of last century the Kirkstall Forge had an international reputation for wrought iron and mechanical engineering and is now owned and managed by GKN Axles Ltd, specialising in the manufacture of heavy-vehicle axles. The low-lying riverside fields between the Forge and Kirkstall Abbey were, until recently, extensively used for the growing of rhubarb, a Yorkshire delicacy reputedly exported to France to help improve the flavour of champagne.

THE ROUTE

Keep ahead past Newlay Bridge. To see the old Newlay Bridge or visit the Abbey Inn leave the towpath by the picnic area at the crossing bridge before the locks (1). The towpath continues down past Newlay Locks and Forge Locks, with Bramley Fall Woods on the right. Alternative paths on the far side of the canal, accessible by foot-bridge, lead into Bramley Fall Woods. Keep ahead past the extensive workshops and sheds of Kirkstall Forge, across the river on the left, to Kirkstall Locks ahead.

Bramley Fall Woods

B6157

Kirkstall Abbey

Kirkstall Lock

①

②

Gotts Park

N

The impressive remains of Kirkstall Abbey

THE ROUTE

Continue past Kirkstall Lock, alongside low riverside fields with the ruins of Kirkstall Abbey to the left, under two bridges carrying heavy traffic into Leeds. (For an exit to Kirkstall traffic lights and buses to central Leeds or back to Shipley take the path to the left (1) past the second bridge to Bramley Hill Road and Bridge Road.) Keep ahead past the old Kirkstall Brewery, under a third bridge (2) known as Amen Corner, continuing alongside and below Gotts Park and Armley Park.

KIRKSTALL ABBEY was founded as a daughter house of Fountains Abbey, North Yorkshire, in 1152, and is generally considered to be the finest and best preserved early Cistercian ruin in the country. Abandoned at the Dissolution in 1539, its roof was quickly stripped of valuable lead, and by the 18th century the ruins were attracting writers and painters such as Horace Walpole and Turner because of their melancholy and picturesque beauty. Now in the ownership of the City of Leeds, it forms the focal point of a delightful area of parkland, whilst part of the old gatehouse forms the excellent Abbey House Museum which has a replica Victorian street and geological and herb gardens.

The magnificent brewery building, now disused, dates from the 1830s when it was built for Benjamin Dawson's Kirkstall Brewery Company brewing a variety of strong, bitter, light and mild ales, porter, stout and Indian pale ales. The beer was sold both for home consumption but also for export – hogsheads of Kirkstall ale were taken by the Leeds-Liverpool Canal and the Aire and Calder Navigation to Goole for trans-shipment by the brewery's own steamships, the SS *Charante* and SS *Kirkstall* to the colonies, especially to New Zealand and Australia.

The third of the three bridges over the canal at Kirkstall carries Wyther Lane over the canal and the sharp bend in the road above at the bridge is known as 'Amen Corner' based on the local legend that monks at their vespers could be heard from here.

Armley Mills - the largest mill in the world when it was built by Benjamin Gott in 1804-5 - now houses the Leeds Industrial Museum

Soon the site of the defunct Kirkstall Power Station is reached, and the Redcote loop crossed by a recently restored footbridge. Continue under the railway line. The huge stone mill building by the weir ahead is Armley Mills, the Leeds Industrial Museum. Access from the towpath is off Canal Road, the next crossing bridge. Turn sharp left down the drive to the museum entrance. Canal and towpath now go under the tall, stone, richly carved viaduct carrying the Leeds-Harrogate railway, and down Spring Garden Locks and Oddy Locks.

Leeds: the Civic Hall (above), the Canal Basin (below) and the Corn Exchange (above right)

THE ROUTE

The canal enters central Leeds under Wellington Road bridge before curving into the city centre above the river in an area still surprisingly green, passing St Anne's Ing and the fine Leeds-Thirsk railway bridge before emerging at the Leeds Canal Basin from where the Leeds-Liverpool Canal locks into the Aire and Calder Navigation – the terminus of the canal.

Cross the footbridge past a variety of canal buildings and warehouses into Water Street. Turn left along Water Street to Bishopgate, then go left again under the railway bridge for City Square and the railway station.

N

Town Hall

Leeds

Canal Basin

Monks Bridge
Ironworks

Index

This guide would not have been possible without the help of Dorian Speakman, who undertook much of the research and re-checking of the towpath and linking routes. The author would also like to thank Mike Clarke for the invaluable information contained in his guide *Around and About the Leeds and Liverpool Canal*.

Thanks are also due to the British Waterways' Leeds-Liverpool area managers for their support and help.